It's another Quality Book from CGP

This book is for anyone doing AQA Modular Science at GCSE.

Whatever subject you're doing it's the same
old story — there are lots of facts and you've just got
to learn them. AQA Modular Science is no different.

Happily this CGP book gives you all that important
information as clearly and concisely as possible.

It's also got some daft bits in to try and make the whole
experience at least vaguely entertaining for you.

The early modules include some material that's also needed in the final exam.
We've stuck this stuff in blue boxes (like this one) so it's easy to find in the book.

What CGP is all about

Our sole aim here at CGP is to produce the highest quality
books — carefully written, immaculately presented and
dangerously close to being funny.

Then we work our socks off to get them out to you
— at the cheapest possible prices.

Early Modules

Contents

(AQA Syllabus reference)

Early Modules # *Contents*

Published by: Coordination Group Publications Ltd
Illustrations by: Sandy Gardner, e-mail: illustrations@sandygardner.co.uk
and Bowser, Colorado USA

Updated by: Suzanne Worthington

ISBN 1 84146 932 7
Groovy Website: www.cgpbooks.co.uk

Printed by Elanders Hindson, Newcastle upon Tyne.
Clipart sources: CorelDRAW and VECTOR.

Proofreading by:
Deborah Dobson
Dominic Hall
James Paul Wallis
David Worthington
Eileen Worthington

Cells

Plant Cells and Animal Cells Have Their Differences

You need to be able to draw these two cells <u>with all the details</u> for each.

Animal Cell

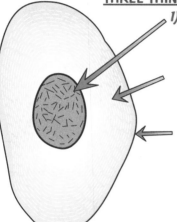

THREE THINGS THEY BOTH HAVE IN COMMON:

1) <u>NUCLEUS</u> contains genetic material that controls what the cell <u>does</u>.

2) <u>CYTOPLASM</u> contains enzymes that <u>speed up</u> biological reactions.

3) <u>CELL MEMBRANE</u> holds the cell together and controls what goes <u>in</u> and <u>out</u>.

Plant Cell

THREE EXTRAS THAT ONLY THE PLANT CELL HAS:

1) <u>RIGID CELL WALL</u> made of <u>cellulose</u>, gives support for the cell.

2) <u>VACUOLE</u> contains <u>cell sap</u>, a weak solution of sugar and salts.

3) <u>CHLOROPLASTS</u> containing <u>chlorophyll</u> for <u>photosynthesis</u>. *Found in the green parts of plants.*

Cells are Specialised for their Function

Most cells are <u>specialised</u> for a specific job, and in the Exam you'll probably have to explain why the cell they've shown you is so good at its job. It's a lot easier if you've <u>already learnt them</u>!

1) Red blood cells are Designed to Carry Oxygen

1) <u>Doughnut</u> shaped to allow maximum oxygen absorption by the <u>haemoglobin</u> they contain. They are <u>doughnut</u> shaped rather than <u>long</u> to allow smooth passage through the <u>capillaries</u>.
2) They don't need a <u>nucleus</u>.

2) Sperm and egg cells are specialised for Reproduction

Egg / Size of sperm in relation to the egg / Sperm

1) The <u>egg</u> cell has huge food reserves to provide nutrition for the developing embryo.
2) When a <u>sperm</u> fuses with the egg, the egg's <u>membrane</u> instantly changes to prevent any more sperm getting in.
3) A long <u>tail</u> gives the sperm the <u>mobility</u> needed for its long journey to find the egg.
4) The sperm also has a <u>short life-span</u> so only the fittest survive the race to the egg.

3) Other Important Examples

There are three other important examples of specialised human cells: <u>WHITE BLOOD CELLS</u>, <u>NEURONES</u> and <u>CELLS IN THE INTESTINES</u>. Look them up and see how they're specialised. (P.10, 29 and 15)

Have you learnt it? — let's see, shall we...

Right then, when you're ready, when you think you've learnt it, <u>cover the page</u> and <u>answer these</u>:
1) Draw an animal cell and a plant cell and put all the labels on them.
2) What three things do plant and animal cells have in common?
3) What are the three differences between them?
4) Draw two specialised human cells and point out their special features.

2

Organs and The Digestive System

Cells / Digestion

Levels of Organisation

This can apply to plants as well as animals, of course.

A group of **SIMILAR CELLS** is called a **TISSUE**.
A group of **DIFFERENT TISSUES** form an **ORGAN**.
A **GROUP OF ORGANS** working together form an **ORGAN SYSTEM**, or even **A WHOLE ORGANISM**.

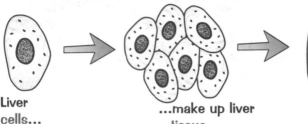

Liver cells... ...make up liver tissue... ...which make up the liver (an organ)... ...and the liver and other organs make the digestive system (an organ system).

Eight Bits of Your Grisly Digestive System to Learn:

Salivary Glands
Produce an enzyme called amylase in the saliva to start the breakdown of starch.

Liver
Where bile is produced.

Small intestine
1) Produces the protease, amylase and lipase enzymes.
2) This is also where the "food" is absorbed into the blood.
3) The inner surface is covered with villi to increase the surface area. It's also very long.

Large intestine
Where excess water is absorbed from the food.

Tongue

Gullet

Stomach
1) It pummels the food with its muscular walls.
2) It produces protease enzymes.
3) It produces hydrochloric acid for two reasons:
   a) To kill bacteria
   b) To give the right pH for the protease enzyme to work (pH 2 - acidic).

Pancreas
Produces the lot: amylase, lipase and the protease enzymes.

Rectum
Where the faeces (made up mainly of indigestible food) are stored before they bid you a fond farewell through the anus.

Have You Learned The Whole Page?
One thing they won't ask you in the Exam is to draw the whole digestion system. BUT they will ask you about any part of it, eg: "What happens in the stomach?", or "What does the pancreas produce?" So in the end, you have to learn the whole thing anyway. Cover the page and draw both diagrams, words and all.

Digestive Enzymes

The human diet is made up of <u>carbohydrates</u>, <u>protiens</u> and <u>fats</u> — and we have <u>three</u> enzymes to break them down. Sadly they all have silly names that can be hard to learn and their '"products of digestion" all have suitably silly names too. Ah well — that's Biology for you.

Enzymes break down *Big Molecules* into *Small Ones*

1) <u>Starch</u>, <u>proteins</u> and <u>fats</u> are <u>BIG</u> molecules which can't pass through cell walls into the blood.
2) <u>Sugars</u>, <u>amino acids</u> and <u>fatty acids/glycerol</u> are <u>much smaller</u> molecules which can pass easily into the blood.
3) <u>Enzymes</u> act as <u>catalysts</u> to break down the <u>BIG molecules</u> into the <u>smaller ones</u>.

1) *Amylase* Converts Starch *into Simple Sugars*

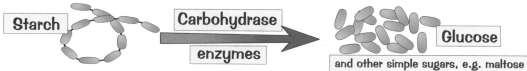

<u>Amylase</u> is produced in <u>three</u> places:

1) The <u>SALIVARY GLANDS</u>
2) The <u>PANCREAS</u>
3) The <u>SMALL INTESTINE</u>

2) *Protease* Converts *Proteins* into *Amino Acids*

Protease is produced in <u>three</u> places:

1) The <u>STOMACH</u> (where it's called *pepsin*)
2) The <u>PANCREAS</u>
3) The <u>SMALL INTESTINE</u>

3) *Lipase* Converts Fats *into* Fatty Acids *and* Glycerol

Lipase is produced in <u>two</u> places:

1) The <u>PANCREAS</u>
2) The <u>SMALL INTESTINE</u>

BILE Neutralises The Stomach Acid *and* Emulsifies Fats

1) Bile is produced in the <u>LIVER</u>. It's <u>stored</u> in the <u>gall bladder</u> before it's released into the small intestine.
2) The hydrochloric acid in the stomach makes the pH <u>too acidic</u> for enzymes to work properly. Bile is <u>alkaline</u> — it <u>neutralises</u> the acid and make conditions alkaline.
   The enzymes in the small intestine <u>work best</u> in these <u>alkaline conditions</u>.
3) It <u>emulsifies fats</u>. In other words it breaks the fat into <u>tiny droplets</u>. This gives a much <u>bigger surface area</u> of fat for the enzyme lipase to work on. Nothing too tricky there.

Yes, you have to know all that stuff too...

OK it's a pretty dreary page of boring facts, but it all counts — you're expected to know <u>every bit</u> of information on this page. So, take a deep breath, <u>read it and learn it</u>, then <u>cover the page</u> and <u>scribble it all down</u>. Then try again, and again... until you can do it. Fun fun fun.

Lungs and Breathing

The Thorax

Learn this diagram really well:

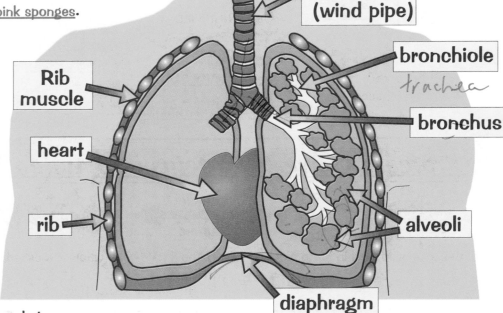

1) The <u>thorax</u> is the top part of your 'body' which is protected by the <u>ribcage</u>.

2) The <u>lungs</u> are like <u>big pink sponges</u>.

3) The <u>trachea</u> splits into two tubes called "<u>bronchi</u>" (each one is "a bronchus"), one going to each lung.

4) The bronchi split into progressively smaller tubes called <u>bronchioles</u>.

5) The bronchioles finally end at small bags called <u>alveoli</u> where the gas exchange takes place.

6) The <u>diaphragm</u> separates the thorax from the abdomen.

Diagram labels: nasal cavity, Gullet (food pipe), trachea (wind pipe), bronchiole, trachea, Rib muscle, bronchus, heart, rib, alveoli, diaphragm

Ventilation

Moving air <u>INTO</u> and <u>OUT OF</u> the lungs is called <u>VENTILATION</u>.

Breathing In...

1) <u>Ribcage</u> moves out.
2) <u>Diaphragm</u> flattens.
3) Air is <u>drawn in</u>.

...and Breathing Out

1) <u>Ribcage</u> moves back in.
2) <u>Diaphragm</u> moves back up
3) Air is <u>forced out</u>.

Stop Huffing and Puffing and just LEARN IT...

No dreary lists of facts this time anyway, just three splendid diagrams to learn.
When you practise repeating diagrams from memory, you don't have to draw them really neatly, just sketch them clear enough to label all the important bits. They would never ask you to draw a really fancy diagram in the Exam, but they will expect you to label one. But the only way to be sure you really know a diagram is to sketch it and label it, <u>all from memory</u>.

Respiration

Respiration is NOT "breathing in and out"

1) Respiration is NOT breathing in and breathing out, as you might think.
2) <u>Respiration</u> actually goes on <u>in every cell in your body</u>.
3) <u>Respiration</u> is the process of <u>converting glucose (a sugar) to energy</u>.
4) It takes place in <u>plants</u> too. All living things "<u>respire</u>". They <u>convert "food" into energy</u>.

> ### RESPIRATION is the process of CONVERTING GLUCOSE TO ENERGY, which goes on in EVERY CELL

5) Energy released by respiration is used for four things:
    a) <u>Build</u> larger molecules from smaller ones   b) enable <u>muscle contraction</u>
    c) maintain a steady <u>body temperature</u>

Aerobic Respiration Needs Plenty of Oxygen

1) <u>Aerobic respiration</u> is what happens if there's <u>plenty of oxygen available</u>.
2) "<u>Aerobic</u>" just means "<u>with oxygen</u>" and it's <u>the ideal way to convert glucose into energy</u>.

You need to learn <u>the word equation</u>:

> ## Glucose + Oxygen → Carbon Dioxide + Water + Energy

Anaerobic Respiration doesn't use Oxygen at all

1) <u>Anaerobic respiration</u> is what happens if there's <u>no oxygen available</u>.
2) "<u>Anaerobic</u>" just means "<u>without oxygen</u>" and it's <u>NOT the best way to convert glucose into energy</u>.

You need to learn <u>the word equation</u>:

> ## Glucose → Energy + Lactic Acid

3) <u>Anaerobic respiration</u> does <u>not produce nearly as much energy</u> as aerobic respiration — but it's useful in emergencies.

Fitness and the Oxygen Debt

1) When you do <u>vigorous exercise</u> and your body can't supply enough <u>oxygen</u> to your muscles they start doing <u>anaerobic respiration</u> instead.
2) This isn't great because the <u>incomplete breakdown</u> of glucose produces a build up of <u>lactic acid</u> in the muscles, which gets <u>painful</u>.
3) The advantage is that at least you can keep on <u>using your muscles</u> for a while longer.
4) After resorting to anaerobic respiration, when you stop you'll have an <u>oxygen debt</u>.
5) In other words you have to "<u>repay</u>" the oxygen which you didn't manage to get to your muscles in time, because your <u>lungs</u>, <u>heart</u> and <u>blood</u> couldn't keep up with the <u>demand earlier on</u>.
6) This means you have to <u>keep breathing hard</u> for a while <u>after you stop</u> to get oxygen into your muscles to get rid of the painful lactic acid.

One Big Deep Breath and LEARN IT...

There are four sections on this page. Learning them well enough to <u>scribble them down</u> from <u>memory</u> isn't so difficult. You don't have to write it out word for word, just make sure you remember the important points about each bit.

The Circulatory System

The circulatory system's main function is to get food and oxygen to every cell in the body.
The diagram shows the basic layout, but make sure you learn the five important points too.

The DOUBLE Circulatory System, actually

① The heart is actually two pumps.
The right side pumps deoxygenated blood to the lungs to collect oxygen.
Then the left side pumps this oxygenated blood around the body.

② Arteries carry blood away from the heart at high pressure.

③ Normally, arteries carry oxygenated blood and veins carry deoxygenated blood.

④ The arteries eventually split off into thousands of tiny capillaries which take blood to every cell in the body.

⑤ The veins then collect the "used" blood and carry it back to the heart at low pressure to be pumped round again.

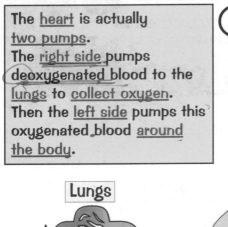

Lungs / Rest of Body

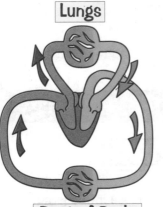

brain, lungs, aorta, pulmonary artery, pulmonary vein, vena cava, heart, liver, gut, kidneys, from lower limbs, to lower limbs

Fish don't have a double circulation system, but all fast-moving creatures like mammals and birds do. If you think about it, it's a mighty clever system to have evolved all by itself. Goodness knows how it ever happened.
I mean how could a single pump system "evolve" into a double one like this? It's got to be all or nothing for it to work hasn't it? That's quite a mutation, to go straight from a single pump heart that pumps to the lungs and then on to the rest of the body, to the double pump system shown above. But then life's full of little mysteries, isn't it.

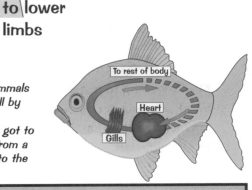

Let's See What You Know then...

At least this stuff on the circulatory system is fairly interesting. Mind you, there are still plenty of picky little details you need to be clear about. And yes, you've guessed it, there's one sure-fire way to check just how clear you are — read it, learn it, then cover the page and reproduce it.
Having to sketch the diagram out again from memory is the only way to really learn it.

The Heart

The heart is made almost entirely of <u>muscle</u>. And it's a <u>double pump</u>.
Visualise this diagram with its <u>bigger side</u> full of <u>red, oxygenated blood</u>, and
its <u>smaller side</u> full of <u>blue, deoxygenated blood</u>, and learn that the <u>left side</u> is <u>bigger</u>.

Learn <u>This</u> Diagram of the Heart <u>with All its Labels</u>

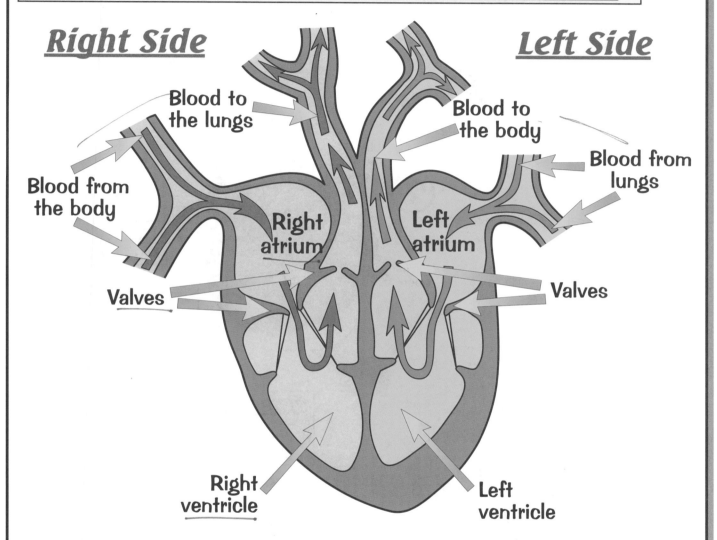

Right Side

Left Side

Blood to
the lungs

Blood to
the body

Blood from
the body

Blood from
lungs

Right
atrium

Left
atrium

Valves

Valves

Right
ventricle

Left
ventricle

Four Extra Details to Delight and Thrill You

1) The <u>right side</u> of the heart receives <u>deoxygenated blood</u> from the body and pumps it only to the <u>lungs</u>, so it has <u>thinner walls</u> than the left side.

2) The <u>left side</u> receives <u>oxygenated blood</u> from the lungs and pumps it out round the <u>whole body</u>, so it has <u>thicker, more muscular walls</u>.

3) The <u>ventricles</u> are <u>much bigger</u> than the <u>atria</u> because they push blood <u>round the body</u>.

4) The <u>valves</u> are for <u>preventing backflow</u> of blood.

OK Let's get to the Heart of the Matter...

They quite often put a diagram of the heart in the Exam and ask you to label parts of it.
There's only one way to be sure you can label it all and that's to learn the diagram until you can
sketch it out, with all the labels, <u>from memory</u>. Also <u>learn</u> the four points at the bottom.

The Pumping Cycle

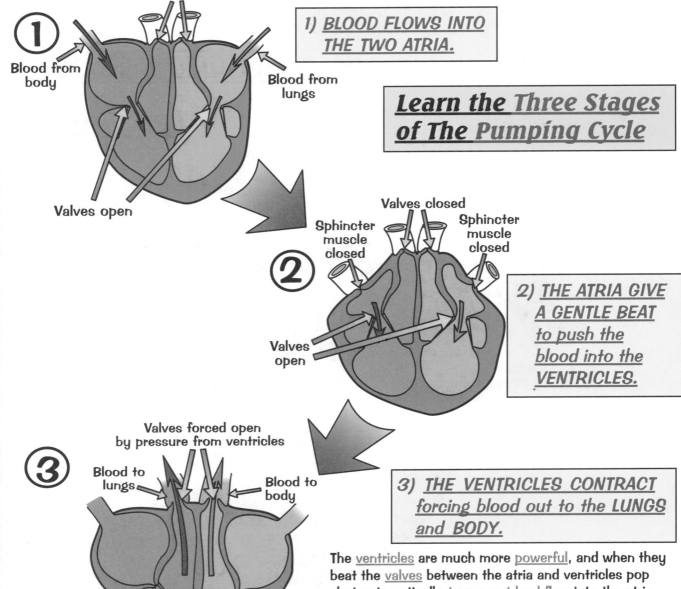

1) BLOOD FLOWS INTO THE TWO ATRIA.

Valves closed

Blood from body

Blood from lungs

Valves open

Learn the Three Stages of The Pumping Cycle

Valves closed

Sphincter muscle closed

Sphincter muscle closed

Valves open

2) THE ATRIA GIVE A GENTLE BEAT to push the blood into the VENTRICLES.

Valves forced open by pressure from ventricles

Blood to lungs

Blood to body

Valves closed automatically

3) THE VENTRICLES CONTRACT forcing blood out to the LUNGS and BODY.

The ventricles are much more powerful, and when they beat the valves between the atria and ventricles pop shut automatically to prevent backflow into the atria. Sphincters wouldn't be strong enough.

As soon as the ventricles relax, valves pop shut to prevent backflow of blood (back into the ventricles) as it is now under a fair bit of pressure in the arteries.

4) THE BLOOD FLOWS DOWN THE ARTERIES, THE ATRIA FILL AGAIN AND THE WHOLE CYCLE STARTS OVER.

If this doesn't get your pulse racing, nothing will...

You need to know the details of each step of the pumping cycle. They will quite cheerfully give you a diagram similar to one of the above and ask you which valves are open or where the blood is flowing etc. etc. Make sure you can sketch out all three diagrams from memory.

Blood Vessels

There are three different types of blood vessel and you need to know all about them:

Arteries Carry Blood Under Pressure

1) Arteries carry oxygenated blood <u>away from the heart</u>.
2) It comes out of the heart at <u>high pressure</u>, so the artery walls have to be <u>strong and elastic</u>.
3) Note how <u>thick</u> the walls are compared to the size of the hole down the middle (the "lumen" — silly name!).

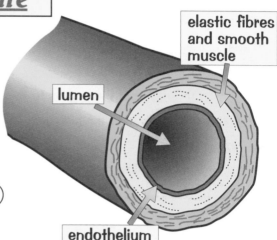

elastic fibres and smooth muscle

lumen

endothelium

Capillaries are Real Small

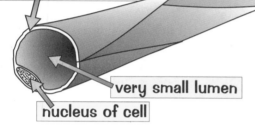

thin endothelium only one cell thick

very small lumen

nucleus of cell

1) Capillaries <u>deliver food and oxygen</u> direct to the body tissues and <u>take waste products away</u>.
2) Their walls are usually <u>only one cell thick</u> to make it easy for stuff <u>to pass in and out of them</u>.
3) They are <u>too small</u> to see.

Veins Take Blood Back to The Heart

1) Veins carry <u>deoxygenated blood</u> back to the heart.
2) The blood is at <u>lower pressure</u> in the veins so <u>the walls do not need to be so thick</u>.
3) They have a <u>bigger lumen</u> than arteries <u>to help blood flow</u>.
4) They also have <u>valves</u> to help keep the blood flowing <u>in the right direction</u>.

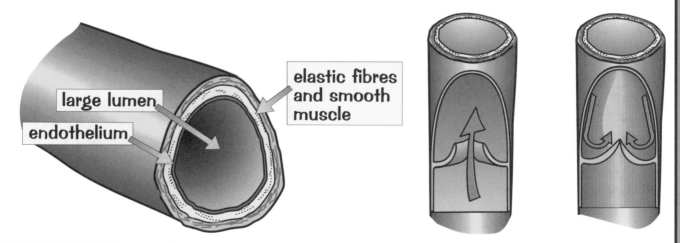

large lumen

endothelium

elastic fibres and smooth muscle

Don't Struggle in Vain...

Let's face it these are mighty easy diagrams to learn. Just make sure you learn the numbered points as well. I reckon it can't take more than two or three attempts before you can scribble out the whole of this page, diagrams and all, <u>entirely from memory</u>. <u>Concentrate on learning the bits you forgot each time</u>, of course. Try it and see how right I am!

Blood

Plasma

This is a pale straw-coloured liquid which <u>carries just about everything</u>:

1) <u>Red</u> and <u>white blood cells</u> and <u>platelets</u>.

2) Digested food products like <u>glucose</u> and <u>amino acids</u>.

3) <u>Carbon dioxide</u> from the organs to the lungs.

4) <u>Urea</u> from the liver to the kidneys.

5) <u>Hormones</u>.

6) <u>Antibodies</u> (including <u>antitoxins</u>) produced by the white blood cells.

Red Blood Cells

1) Their job is to <u>carry oxygen</u> from the lungs to all the cells in the body.

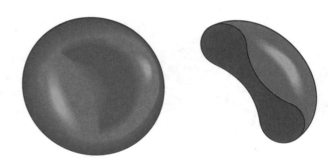

2) They have a <u>flying doughnut shape</u> to give <u>maximum surface area</u> for <u>absorbing oxygen</u>.

White Blood Cells

1) Their main role is <u>defence against disease</u>.

2) They have a <u>big nucleus</u>.

3) They <u>gobble up unwelcome microorganisms</u>.

4) They produce <u>antibodies</u> to fight bacteria.

5) They produce <u>antitoxins</u> to neutralise the toxins produced by bacteria.

Platelets

1) These are <u>small fragments of cells</u>.

2) They have <u>no nucleus</u>.

3) They <u>help the blood to clot</u> at a wound.
   (So basically they just float about waiting for accidents to happen!)

More Blood, Sweat and Tears...

Do the same as usual — learn the facts <u>until you can write them down from memory</u>.

Just in case you think all this formal learning is a waste of time, how do you think you'd get on with these typical Exam questions if you didn't <u>learn</u> it all first?

<u>Three typical Exam questions</u>:

1) What is the function of blood plasma? (4 marks)

2) What do white blood cells do?   (3 marks)

3) Explain the shape of red blood cells? (2 marks)

Disease in Humans

The Two Types of Microorganism: Bacteria and Viruses

Microorganisms can get inside you and make you feel ill. There are two main types:

Bacteria are Very Small Living Cells

1) These are <u>very small cells</u>, (about 1/100th the size of your body cells), which reproduce rapidly inside your body.

2) They make you <u>feel ill</u> by doing <u>two</u> things:
   - a) <u>damaging your cells</u>
   - b) <u>producing toxins</u>.

3) Don't forget that some bacteria are <u>useful</u> if they're in the <u>right place</u>, like in your digestive system.

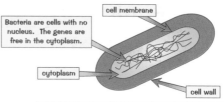

Bacteria are cells with no nucleus. The genes are free in the cytoplasm.

cell membrane

cytoplasm

cell wall

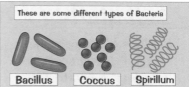

These are some different types of Bacteria

Bacillus   Coccus   Spirillum

Viruses are not cells — they're much smaller

1) These are <u>not cells</u>. They are <u>very very small</u>, about 1/100th the size of a bacterium.

2) They are no more than a <u>coat of protein</u> around a <u>DNA strand</u>.

3) They make you feel ill by <u>damaging your cells</u>.

4) They <u>replicate themselves</u> by invading the <u>nucleus</u> of a <u>living</u> cell and using the <u>DNA</u> it contains to produce many <u>copies</u> of themselves.

5) The cell then <u>bursts</u>, releasing all the new viruses.

6) In this way they can reproduce <u>very quickly</u>.

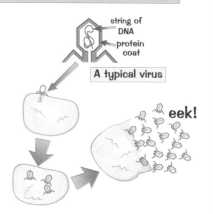

string of DNA

protein coat

A typical virus

eek!

The Body has Three ways of Defending Itself

<u>Diseases</u> can be caused when <u>microorganisms</u> such as certain <u>bacteria</u> and <u>viruses</u> enter the body. Disease is more likely to occur if large numbers of microorganisms enter the body as a result of <u>unhygienic conditions</u> or contact with <u>infected people</u>. However we do have some <u>defences</u>.

1) The Skin and Eyes are Barriers

<u>Undamaged skin</u> is a very effective barrier against microorganisms. <u>Eyes</u> produce a chemical which <u>kills bacteria</u> on the surface of the eye.

2) The Blood Clots to Seal Cuts

As well as stopping your blood from gushing out and making a mess, the clotting also <u>prevents</u> any passing microorganisms from entering your body through your <u>skin</u>.

3) The Breathing System Produces Sticky Mucus

The whole <u>respiratory tract</u> (nasal passage, trachea and lungs) is lined with <u>mucus</u> and <u>cilia</u> which catch <u>dust</u> and <u>bacteria</u> before they reach the lungs.

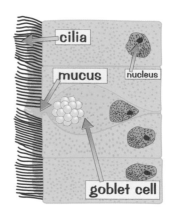

cilia

mucus

nucleus

goblet cell

It's Grisly Stuff, but worth learning just the Same...

Make sure you can <u>draw</u> and <u>label</u> a bacteria and a virus. Then cover up the bottom of the page — check you can <u>list</u> the body's three methods of defence and <u>describe</u> how they work. Blee.

Fighting Disease

Once microorganisms have entered our bodies they will reproduce rapidly unless they are destroyed. Your "immune system" does just that, and white blood cells are the most important part of it.

Your Immune System: White blood cells

They travel around in your blood and crawl into every part of you, constantly patrolling for microorganisms. When they come across an invading microorganism they have three lines of attack:

1) Consuming Them

White blood cells can engulf foreign cells and "ingest" (absorb) them.

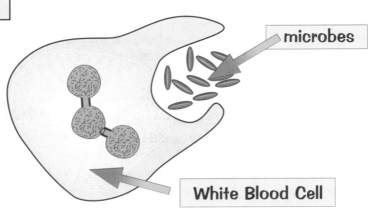

microbes

White Blood Cell

2) Producing Antibodies

When your white blood cells come across a foreign cell they will start to produce chemicals called antibodies to kill the new invading cells.

The antibodies produced rapidly and flow all round the body to kill all similar bacteria or viruses. If the same microorganisms are encountered in the future the same antibodies can be produced quickly making the person immune.

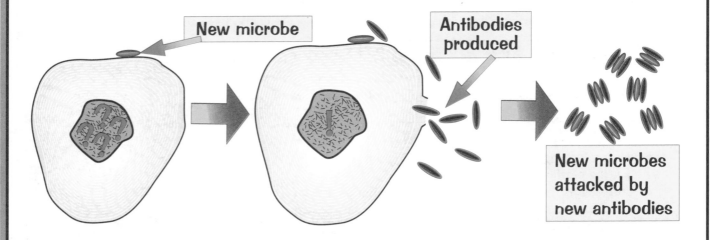

New microbe

Antibodies produced

New microbes attacked by new antibodies

3) Producing Antitoxins

Antitoxins counter the effect of any poisons (toxins) produced by the invading bacteria.

Fighting Disease

Immunisation — producing antibodies beforehand

1) Once your <u>white cells</u> have produced <u>antibodies</u> to tackle a <u>new strain</u> of bacteria or virus you are said to have developed "<u>natural immunity</u>" to it.

2) That means if you get infected by the <u>same microorganisms</u> in future they'll be killed <u>immediately</u> by the <u>antibodies</u> you already have for them, and you <u>won't get ill</u>.

3) The trouble is when a <u>new</u> microorganism appears, it takes your white cells <u>a few days</u> to produce the antibodies to deal with them and in that time you can get <u>very ill</u>.

4) There are <u>plenty of diseases</u> which can make you <u>very ill indeed</u> (e.g. polio, tetanus, measles) and only <u>immunisation</u> stops you getting them.

5) Immunisation involves injecting <u>dead microorganisms</u> into you. This causes your body to produce <u>antibodies</u> to attack them, even though they're dead. They can do no <u>harm</u> to you because they're dead.

6) If <u>live microorganisms of the same type</u> appeared <u>after that</u> however, they'd be <u>killed immediately</u> by the antibodies which you have already developed against them. Cool.

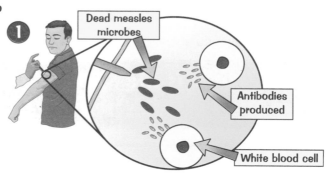

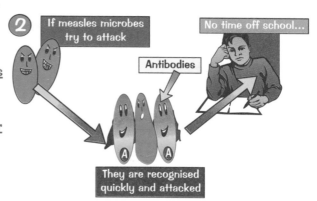

Antibiotics kill Bacteria but NOT Viruses

1) <u>Antibiotics</u> are <u>drugs</u> that kill <u>bacteria</u> without killing your own body cells.

2) They are <u>very useful</u> for clearing up infections that your body is having <u>trouble</u> with.

3) However they don't kill <u>viruses</u>. <u>Flu and colds</u> are caused by <u>viruses</u> and basically, <u>you're on your own</u>, pal.

4) There are <u>no drugs</u> to kill <u>viruses</u> and you just have to <u>wait</u> for your body to deal with them and <u>suffer</u> in the meantime.

5) Still, it's better than being bitten by a rat flea.

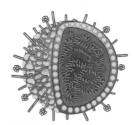

A horrid Flu Virus

An even more horrid Rat Flea

Don't let Revision make you sick — just learn and enjoy...

Don't let the big diagrams fool you — this stuff's complicated and needs careful learning. Make sure you <u>know all the details</u> of your body's natural immune system and the process of immunisation used to prevent disease. Make a list of <u>numbered points</u> for each page and keep learning them <u>till you know the lot</u>.

Diffusion

Don't be put off by the fancy word

"Diffusion" is really simple. It's just the <u>gradual net movement of particles</u> from places where there are <u>lots of them</u> to places where there are <u>fewer of them</u>. That's all it is — it's just the <u>natural tendency</u> for stuff to <u>spread out</u>.

Unfortunately you also have to <u>learn</u> the fancy way of saying the same thing, which is this:

> *DIFFUSION is the NET MOVEMENT OF PARTICLES from a region of HIGH CONCENTRATION to an area of LOW CONCENTRATION*

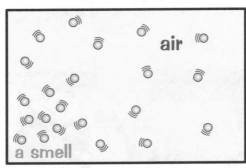  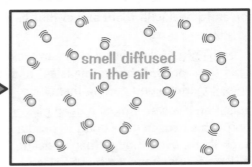

Diffusion Through Cell membranes is kind of clever...

Cell membranes are kind of clever because they hold everything <u>inside</u> the cell, <u>but</u>, they let stuff <u>in and out</u> as well. Only very <u>small molecules</u> can diffuse through cell membranes though — things like <u>sugar</u>, <u>water</u> or <u>ions</u>.

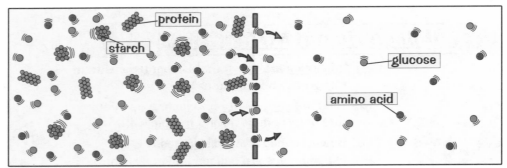

1) Notice that <u>big molecules</u> like <u>starch</u> or <u>proteins</u> can't diffuse through cell membranes — they could quite cheerfully ask you exactly that in the Exam.
2) Just like with diffusion in air, particles flow through the cell membrane from where there's a <u>high concentration</u> (a lot of them) to where there's a <u>low concentration</u> (not such a lot of them).
3) The <u>rate of diffusion</u> is directly affected by the concentration gradient — "<u>the GREATER the difference in concentration the FASTER the rate of diffusion</u>". Now don't you forget that.

So, how much do you know about diffusion?

Yeah sure it's a pretty book but actually the big idea is to <u>learn</u> all the stuff that's in it.
So learn this page until you can answer these questions <u>without having to look back</u>:

1) Write down the fancy definition for diffusion, and then say what it means in your own words.
2) Explain what will and won't diffuse through cell membranes. In which direction do things diffuse?
3) Write down the rule governing the rate of diffusion.

Diffusion

The Small Molecules Can Then Diffuse into the Blood

These molecules (glucose, amino acids, fatty acids and glycerol) are then <u>small enough</u> to <u>diffuse into the blood</u>.

In fact, these molecules will only "diffuse" into the blood with the help of <u>special cells</u> because the <u>concentration gradient</u> is the wrong way.

They then <u>travel to where they're needed</u>, and then <u>diffuse out again</u>. It's all clever stuff.

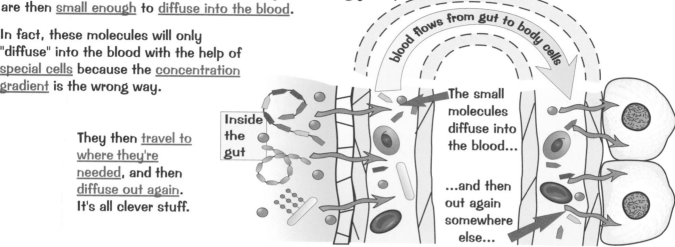

blood flows from gut to body cells

Inside the gut

The small molecules diffuse into the blood...

...and then out again somewhere else...

Villi Provide a Really Big Surface Area

The inside of the <u>small intestine</u> is covered in millions and millions of these tiny little projections called <u>villi</u>.

They increase the surface area in a big way so that digested food is <u>absorbed</u> much more quickly into the <u>blood</u>.

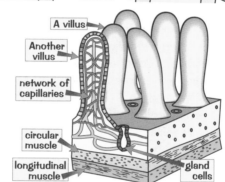

A villus
Another villus
network of capillaries
circular muscle
longitudinal muscle
gland cells

Gas Exchange in the Lungs

The <u>lungs</u> contain millions and millions of little air sacs called <u>ALVEOLI</u> (see diagram opposite) which are specialised to maximise the <u>diffusion</u> of oxygen and CO_2. The <u>alveoli</u> are an ideal <u>exchange surface</u>. They have an <u>enormous surface area</u> (about 70m² in total).

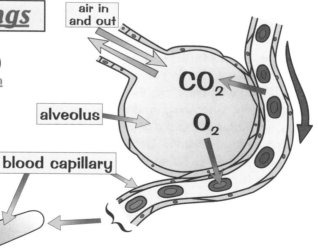

air in and out

CO_2

O_2

alveolus

blood capillary

thin endothelium only one cell thick

very small lumen

nucleus of cell

To give you an idea of the size of things here — the capillaries are normally <u>too small</u> to see.

This is a very Easy Page To Learn...

The big idea is that you should <u>understand and remember</u> what goes on and why it all works so well. A clear visual image in your head of these diagrams makes it a lot easier.
<u>Learn</u> the diagrams, words and all, until you can sketch them out <u>entirely from memory</u>.

Revision Summary for Module One

Phew, there's a lot of stuff to learn in Module One. And it's all that grisly "open heart surgery" type stuff too, with all those gory diagrams. Mind you, it's all fairly straightforward and factual — nothing difficult to understand, just lots of facts to learn. And lots of gory diagrams. You know the big plan with these questions though. Keep practising till you can whizz them all off without a moment's hesitation on any of them. It's a nice trick if you can do it.

1) Sketch a typical animal cell with labels adding a brief description for each one.
2) Sketch three different animal cells and describe their specialised functions.
3) Give an animal example of this sequence: cells → tissues → organ → organ-system → organism.
4) Sketch the diagram below adding the names for parts A to H.
5) Write down at least two details for each of the labelled parts.

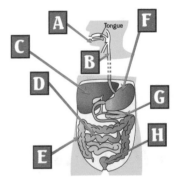

6) What *exactly* do enzymes do in the digestive system?
7) List the three main types of digestive enzymes, which foods they act on, and what they produce.
8) Where is bile produced and stored? What does it do?
9) Draw a diagram of the breathing system, showing all your breathing equipment.
10) What is 'ventilation'? Describe the stages of the process.
11) Where are alveoli found? How big are they and what are they for? Give four features.
12) What is 'respiration'? Give a proper definition.
13) What is "aerobic respiration"? Give the word equation for it.
14) What is "anaerobic respiration"? Give the word equation for what happens in our bodies.
15) Why can your muscles hurt during vigorous exercise? What is the oxygen debt?
16) Draw a diagram of the human circulatory system: heart, lungs, arteries, veins, etc.
17) Explain why it is a *double* circulatory system, and describe the pressure and oxygen content of the blood in each bit. What are the big words for saying if the blood has oxygen in or not?
18) Draw a full diagram of the heart with all the labels. Explain how the two halves differ.
19) How do ventricles and atria compare, and why? What are the valves for?
20) Describe briefly with diagrams the three stages of the pumping cycle for the heart.
21) Sketch an artery, a capillary, and a vein, with labels, and explain the features of all three.
22) Sketch a red blood cell and a white blood cell and give details about each.
23) Sketch some blood plasma. List all the things that are carried in the plasma (around 10).
24) Sketch some platelets. What do they do all day?
25) How exactly do bacteria make you feel ill? Sketch a bacterium.
26) What do viruses do inside you to replicate? Illustrate with sketches.
27) Describe the body's three defences to keep microorganisms out.
28) What is meant by your 'immune system'? What is the most important part of it?
29) List the three ways that white blood cells deal with invading microorganisms.
30) Give full details of the process of immunisation. How does it work?
31) What are antibiotics? What will they work on and what will they not work on?
32) Give the strict definition of diffusion.
33) Why are cell membranes kinda clever?
34) What will and won't diffuse through cell membranes?
35) Name and describe two places where diffusion occurs in the human body.

Plant Cells

Basic Stuff

Most Cells have:

1) <u>Nucleus</u>
controls what the cell <u>does</u>.

2) <u>Cytoplasm</u>
where the <u>chemical reactions</u> happen.

3) <u>Cell membrane</u>
holds the cell together and <u>controls</u> what goes <u>in and out</u>.

Only Plants have:

1) <u>Rigid cell wall</u>
made of <u>cellulose</u>, gives <u>support</u> for the cell.

2) <u>Vacuole</u>
Contains <u>cell sap</u>, a weak solution of sugar and salts.

3) <u>Green chloroplasts</u>
containing <u>chlorophyll</u> for <u>photosynthesis</u>.

Specialised Plant Cells

Most cells are <u>specialised</u> for a specific job, and in the Exam you'll probably have to explain why the cell they've shown you is so good at its job. It's a lot easier if you've <u>already learnt them</u>...

1) Palisade Leaf Cells are Designed for Photosynthesis

1) Packed with <u>chloroplasts</u> for <u>photosynthesis</u>.
2) <u>Tall</u> shape means a lot of <u>surface area</u> exposed down the side for <u>absorbing CO</u>$_2$ from the air in the leaf.
3) Tall shape also means a good chance of <u>light</u> hitting a <u>chloroplast</u> before it reaches the bottom of the cell.

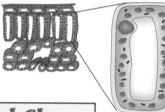

2) Guard Cells are Designed to Open and Close

1) Special <u>kidney shape</u> which <u>opens</u> and <u>closes</u> the stomata (a single pore is a stoma) as the cells go <u>turgid</u> or <u>flaccid</u>.
2) <u>Thin</u> outer walls and <u>thickened</u> inner walls make this opening and closing function work properly.
3) They're also <u>sensitive to light</u> and <u>close at night</u> to conserve water.

3) Xylem Cells are Designed for Water Transport

1) Xylem tissue forms a <u>xylem tube</u> made up of <u>dead cells</u> joined end to end with <u>no end walls</u> between them.
2) The side walls are <u>strong and stiff</u> to give the plant <u>support</u>.
3) The xylem tubes carry <u>water and minerals</u> from the <u>roots</u> up to the <u>leaves</u> in the transpiration stream.

(You'll learn more about the phloem tubes in later – bet you can't wait.)

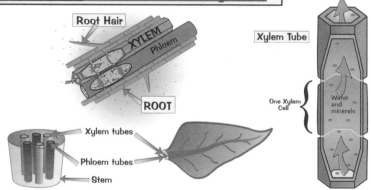

Let's See What You've Learned Then...

This is a pretty straightforward page of information. You need to make sure you know all the diagrams with all the labels and also the numbered points for each.
Practise until you can <u>scribble</u> the whole lot down <u>from memory</u>.

Basic Plant Structure

You have to know all these parts of the plant and what they do:

The Five Different Bits of a Plant all do Different Jobs

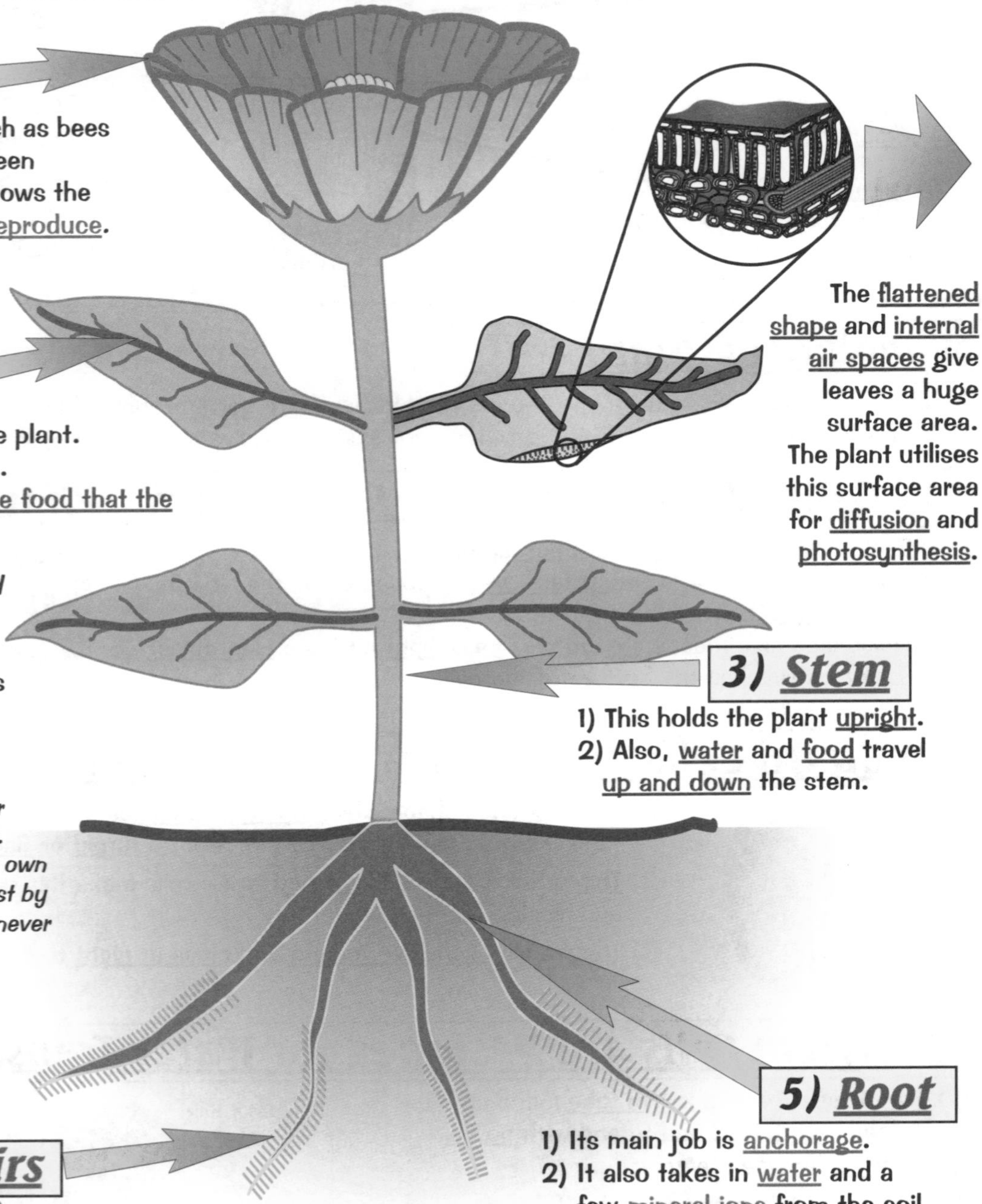

1) Flower

This attracts insects such as bees which carry pollen between different plants. This allows the plants to pollinate and reproduce.

The flattened shape and internal air spaces give leaves a huge surface area. The plant utilises this surface area for diffusion and photosynthesis.

2) Leaf

It produces food for the plant. I'll say it again, listen.... The leaf produces all the food that the plant needs.

Plants do not take food from the soil. Plants make all their own food in their leaves using photosynthesis.

(That's a bit of a shocker when you think about it. Imagine making all your own food under your skin just by lying in the sun — and never having to eat at all!)

3) Stem

1) This holds the plant upright.
2) Also, water and food travel up and down the stem.

5) Root

1) Its main job is anchorage.
2) It also takes in water and a few mineral ions from the soil. But mostly just water. REMEMBER, plants do not take 'food' in from the soil.

4) Root hairs

These give a big surface area to absorb water and ions from the soil.

The Big Idea is to LEARN All That...

Everything on this page is there to be learnt because it's very likely to come up in your Exams. This is pretty basic stuff, but it can still catch you out if you don't learn it properly. For example: "What is the main function of the root?". Too many people answer that with "Taking food in from the soil" — Eeek! LEARN these facts. They all count. They're all worth marks in the Exam. Practise until you can sketch the diagram and scribble down all the details, without looking back.

Photosynthesis

Photosynthesis *Produces* Glucose *from Sunlight*

1) <u>Photosynthesis</u> is the process that produces '<u>food</u>' in plants. The 'food' it produces is <u>glucose</u>.
2) Photosynthesis takes place in the <u>leaves</u> of all <u>green plants</u> — this is what leaves are for.

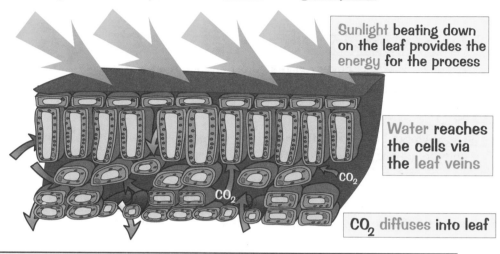

Sunlight beating down on the leaf provides the energy for the process

Water **reaches** the cells via the <u>leaf veins</u>

CO_2 diffuses into leaf

Three Features:
1) Leaves are <u>thin</u> and <u>flat</u> to provide a <u>big surface area</u> to catch <u>lots</u> of sunlight.

2) The <u>palisade</u> cells are <u>near the top</u> of the leaf and are packed with <u>chloroplasts</u>.

3) <u>Guard cells</u> control the movement of <u>gases</u> into and out of the leaf.

Learn the Equation for Photosynthesis:

$$\text{Carbon dioxide} + \text{Water} \xrightarrow[\text{chlorophyll}]{\text{LIGHT ENERGY}} \text{glucose} + \text{oxygen}$$

Four Things are Needed for Photosynthesis to Happen:

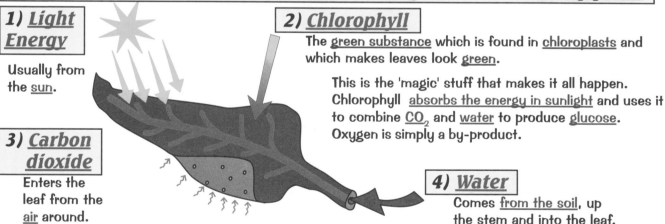

1) Light Energy

Usually from the <u>sun</u>.

2) Chlorophyll

The <u>green substance</u> which is found in <u>chloroplasts</u> and which makes leaves look <u>green</u>.

This is the 'magic' stuff that makes it all happen. Chlorophyll <u>absorbs the energy in sunlight</u> and uses it to combine <u>CO_2</u> and <u>water</u> to produce <u>glucose</u>. Oxygen is simply a by-product.

3) Carbon dioxide

Enters the leaf from the <u>air</u> around.

4) Water

Comes <u>from the soil</u>, up the stem and into the leaf.

Glucose is used for Respiration

1) Plants manufacture <u>glucose</u> in their <u>leaves</u>. They then use some of the glucose initially for <u>respiration</u>.
2) This <u>releases energy</u> which enables them to <u>convert</u> the rest of the glucose into various <u>other useful substances</u> which they can use to <u>build new cells</u> and <u>grow</u>.
3) To produce some of these substances they also need to <u>gather</u> a few <u>minerals</u> from the soil.
4) Glucose can be turned into <u>insoluble starch</u> and <u>stored</u> for use when photosynthesis isn't happening, like in the winter. It's stored in the roots, stems and leaves.

Live and Learn...

What you've got to do now is learn everything on this page. Photosynthesis is a 'dead cert' for the Exams. Just keep learning the <u>diagrams and points</u> until you can <u>cover the page</u> and write them all down <u>from memory</u>. Only then will you really <u>know it all</u>.

The Rate of Photosynthesis

The rate of photosynthesis is affected by three factors:

1) THE AMOUNT OF LIGHT

The chlorophyll uses light energy to perform photosynthesis. It can only do it as fast as the light energy is arriving. Chlorophyll actually only absorbs the red and blue ends of the visible light spectrum, but not the green light in the middle, which is reflected back. This is why the plant looks green.

2) THE AMOUNT OF CARBON DIOXIDE

CO_2 and water are the raw materials. Water is never really in short supply in a plant but only 0.03% of the air around is CO_2 so it's actually pretty scarce as far as plants are concerned.

3) THE TEMPERATURE

Chlorophyll is like an enzyme so it works best when it's warm but not too hot. The rate of photosynthesis depends on how 'happy' the chlorophyll enzyme is: WARM but not too hot.

Three Important Graphs For Rate of Photosynthesis

At any given time one or other of the above three factors will be the limiting factor which is keeping the photosynthesis down at the rate it is.

1) Not Enough LIGHT Slows Down the Rate of Photosynthesis

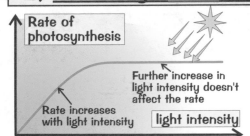

Rate of photosynthesis

Further increase in light intensity doesn't affect the rate

Rate increases with light intensity

light intensity

1) As the light level is raised, the rate of photosynthesis increases steadily but only up to a certain point.

2) Beyond that, it won't make any difference because then it'll be either the temperature or the CO2 level which is the limiting factor.

2) Too Little CARBON DIOXIDE also Slows it Down

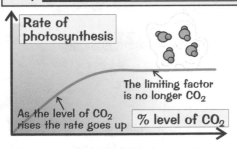

Rate of photosynthesis

The limiting factor is no longer CO_2

As the level of CO_2 rises the rate goes up

% level of CO_2

1) As with light intensity the amount of CO_2 will only increase the rate of photosynthesis up to a point. After this the graph flattens out showing that CO_2 is no longer the limiting factor.

2) As long as light and CO_2 are in plentiful supply then the factor limiting photosynthesis must be temperature.

3) The TEMPERATURE has to be Just Right

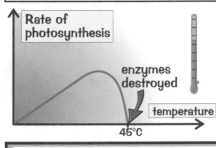

Rate of photosynthesis

enzymes destroyed

temperature

45°C

1) Note that you can't really have too much light or CO_2. The temperature however must not get too high or it destroys the chlorophyll enzymes.

2) This happens at about 45°C (which is pretty hot for outdoors, though greenhouses can get that hot if you're not careful).

3) Usually, though, if the temperature is the limiting factor it's because it's too low, and things need warming up a bit.

Revision — life isn't all fun and sunshine...

There are three limiting factors, a graph for each and an explanation of why the graphs level off or stop abruptly. Cover the page and practise recalling all these details, until you can do it.

Diffusion

Don't be put off by the fancy word

You've done diffusion already in module one, but here it is again in module two, so no excuse for making a pig's dinner of it this time... "Diffusion" is just the <u>gradual movement</u> of particles from places where there are <u>lots</u> of them to places where there are <u>fewer</u> of them.

That's all it is — <u>it's just the natural tendency for stuff to spread out</u>.

Unfortunately you also have to <u>learn</u> the fancy way of saying the same thing, which is this:

> **DIFFUSION** *is the* **NET MOVEMENT OF PARTICLES** *from a region of* **HIGH CONCENTRATION** *to an area of* **LOW CONCENTRATION**

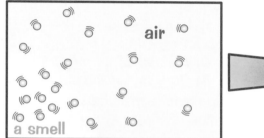
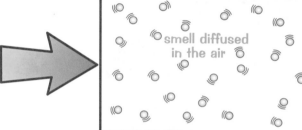

Diffusion of Gases in Leaves is vital for Photosynthesis

The <u>simplest type</u> of diffusion is where different gases diffuse through each other, like when a weird smell spreads out through the air in a room. Diffusion of gases also happens in <u>leaves</u> and they'll very likely put it in your Exam. So learn it now:

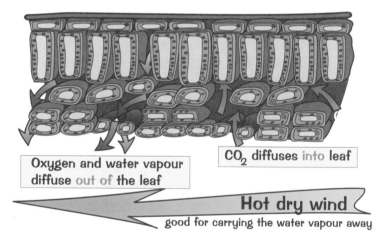

Oxygen and water vapour diffuse out of the leaf

CO₂ diffuses into leaf

Hot dry wind
good for carrying the water vapour away

For photosynthesis to happen, <u>carbon dioxide</u> gas has to get <u>inside</u> the leaves.
It does this by diffusion through the tiny little holes under the leaf called <u>stomata</u>.

At the same time <u>water vapour</u> and <u>oxygen</u> diffuse <u>out</u> through the same tiny little holes.

The water vapour escapes by diffusion because there's a lot of it <u>inside</u> the leaf and less of it in the <u>air outside</u>. This diffusion causes <u>transpiration</u> and it goes <u>quicker</u> when the air around the leaf is kept <u>dry</u> — ie: transpiration is quickest in <u>hot</u>, <u>dry</u>, <u>windy</u> conditions — and don't you forget it!

Diffusion — Silent but deadly...

Yeah sure it's a pretty book but actually the big idea is to <u>learn</u> all the stuff that's in it.
So learn this page until you can answer these questions <u>without having to look back</u>:

1) Write down the fancy definition for diffusion, and then say what it means in your own words.
2) Draw the cross-section of the leaf with arrows to show which way the three gases diffuse.
3) What weather conditions make the diffusion of water vapour out of the leaf go fastest?

The Transpiration Stream

Transpiration is the loss of water from the Plant

1) It's caused by the <u>evaporation</u> of water from <u>inside</u> the <u>leaves</u>. Most of the action involves the <u>stomata</u> shown on the following page.

2) This creates a <u>slight shortage</u> of water in the leaf which <u>draws more water up</u> from the rest of the plant which <u>in turn</u> draws more up from the <u>roots</u>.

3) It has <u>two beneficial effects</u>:   a) it <u>transports minerals</u> from the soil   b) it <u>cools</u> the plant.

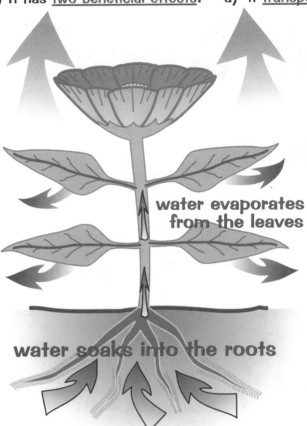

water evaporates from the leaves

water soaks into the roots

The uptake of <u>water</u> and <u>minerals</u> happens almost entirely at the <u>root hairs</u>.

Four factors which affect it

The <u>rate of transpiration</u> is affected by <u>four things</u>:

    1) Amount of <u>light</u>
    2) <u>Temperature</u>
    3) Amount of <u>air movement</u>
    4) <u>Humidity</u> of the surrounding air

It's surely obvious that the <u>biggest</u> rate of transpiration occurs in <u>hot</u>, <u>dry</u>, <u>windy</u>, conditions
    ie: perfect clothes-drying weather.

By contrast a <u>cool</u>, <u>cloudy</u>, <u>muggy</u>, <u>day</u> with <u>no wind</u> will produce <u>minimum transpiration</u>.

This constant stream of water has the advantage of transporting <u>vital minerals</u> from the <u>soil</u> into the roots and then all around the plant.

Leaves Help to Limit Transpiration

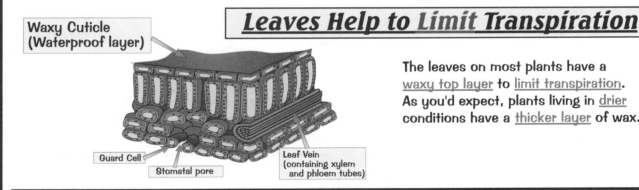

Waxy Cuticle (Waterproof layer)

Guard Cell

Stomatal pore

Leaf Vein (containing xylem and phloem tubes)

The leaves on most plants have a <u>waxy top layer</u> to <u>limit transpiration</u>. As you'd expect, plants living in <u>drier</u> conditions have a <u>thicker layer</u> of wax.

It helps if you're quick on the uptake...

There's quite a lot of information on this page. You could try learning the numbered points, but you'll find a better plan is to do a 'mini-essay' on transpiration and write down everything you can think of. Then look back to see what you've forgotten. Then do it again! <u>Till you get it all</u>.

The Cells' Role in Transpiration

Root Hair Cell

1) The cells on plant roots grow into long hairs' which stick out into the soil.

2) This gives the plant a big surface area for absorbing water and minerals from the soil.

3) Water is taken in almost entirely at the root hairs.

4) Minerals are also taken in at the root hairs.

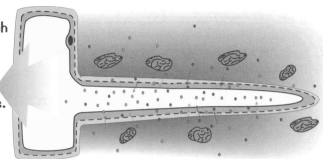

Water Pressure Provides Support for Younger Plants

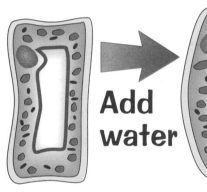 

Add water

1) When a plant is well watered, all its cells will draw water into themselves causing high internal pressure.

2) The contents of the cell start to push against the cell wall, kind of like a balloon in a shoebox, and thereby give support to the plant tissues.

3) Leaves are entirely supported by this pressure.
   We know this because if there's no water in the soil, a plant starts to wilt and the leaves droop.
   This is because the cells start to lose water and thus lose this pressure.

Stomata are Pores which Open and Close Automatically

1) Stomata close automatically when supplies of water from the roots start to dry up.

2) The guard cells control this. When water is scarce, they become soft, and they change shape, which closes the stomatal pores.

3) This prevents any more water being lost, but also stops CO_2 getting in, so the photosynthesis stops as well.

   Limiting water loss is especially important in younger plants as water pressure is their main method of support.

Cells full, pore opens

Cells soft, pore closes

Spend some time poring over these facts...

Three spiffing diagrams and a few simple features. What could be easier? Check the clock and give yourself five minutes of intense active learning to see how much you can learn. 'Intense active learning' means covering the page and scribbling down the details, but don't take 5 minutes drawing out a neat diagram of a root hair — that's just a waste of precious time.

Transport Systems in Plants

Plants need to transport various things around inside themselves. They have tubes for it.

Phloem and Xylem Vessels Transport Different Things

1) Flowering plants have <u>two</u> separate sets of <u>tubes</u> for transporting stuff around the plant.
2) <u>Both</u> sets of tubes go to <u>every part</u> of the plant, but they are totally <u>separate</u>.
3) They usually run <u>alongside</u> each other.

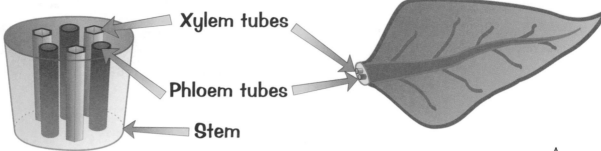

Xylem tubes

Phloem tubes

Stem

Water and food

Phloem Tubes transport Food:

1) Made of <u>living cells</u> with <u>perforated end-plates</u> to allow stuff to flow through.
2) They transport <u>food</u> made in the <u>leaves</u> to <u>all other parts</u> of the plant, in <u>both directions</u>.
3) They carry <u>sugars</u>, <u>fats</u>, <u>proteins</u> etc. to <u>growing regions</u> in <u>shoot tips</u> and <u>root tips</u> and to/from <u>storage organs</u> in the <u>roots</u>.

Xylem Tubes take water UP:

1) Made of <u>dead cells</u> joined end to end with <u>no end walls</u> between them.
2) The side walls are <u>strong and stiff</u> and contain <u>lignin</u>. This gives the plant <u>support</u>.
3) They carry <u>water and minerals</u> from the <u>roots</u> up to the leaves in the transpiration stream.

Water and minerals

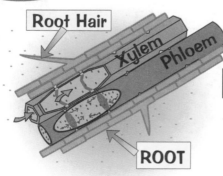

Root Hair

Xylem

Phloem

ROOT

The Phloem and Xylem extend into the Roots

1) The <u>phloem</u> carries substances down to the <u>roots</u> for <u>growth</u> or for <u>storage</u> and may later carry them <u>back up again</u>.
2) The <u>xylem</u> carries <u>water and minerals</u>, (which are taken in by the roots), <u>up</u> to the stem and into the leaves.

Well that seems to be about the top and bottom of it...

This is an easy page. There are important differences between xylem and phloem tubes. Make sure you know all the numbered points on this page, and the diagrams. Then cover the page and scribble it all down with detailed sketches of the diagrams. Then do it again, <u>until you get it all</u>.

Osmosis

Osmosis _is a_ _Special Case_ _of Diffusion, that's all_

> <u>OSMOSIS</u> is the <u>movement of water molecules</u> across a <u>partially permeable membrane</u> from a region of <u>HIGH WATER CONCENTRATION</u> to a region of <u>LOW WATER CONCENTRATION</u>.

1) A <u>partially permeable membrane</u> is just one with <u>really small holes</u> in it. So small, in fact, that <u>only water</u> molecules can pass through them, and bigger molecules like <u>glucose</u> can't.

2) <u>Visking tubing</u> is a partially permeable membrane that you should learn the <u>name</u> of.
It's also called <u>dialysis tubing</u> because it's used in <u>kidney dialysis machines</u>.

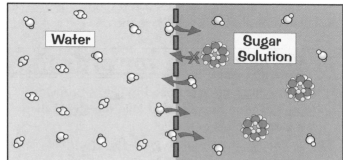

3) The water molecules actually pass <u>both ways</u> through the membrane in a <u>two-way traffic</u>.

4) But because there are <u>more on one side</u> than the other there's a steady <u>net flow</u> into the region with <u>fewer</u> water molecules, ie: into the <u>stronger solution</u> (of glucose).

5) This causes the <u>glucose-rich</u> region to fill up with <u>water</u>. The water acts like it's trying to <u>dilute</u> it, so as to 'even up' the concentration either side of the membrane.

Net movement of water molecules

Two Osmosis Experiments — Favourites for the Exams

① *Potato Tubes*

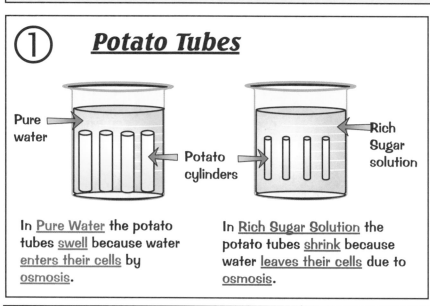

Pure water

Potato cylinders

Rich Sugar solution

In <u>Pure Water</u> the potato tubes <u>swell</u> because water <u>enters their cells</u> by <u>osmosis</u>.

In <u>Rich Sugar Solution</u> the potato tubes <u>shrink</u> because water <u>leaves their cells</u> due to <u>osmosis</u>.

② *Visking Tubing*

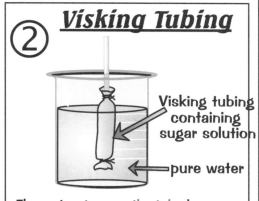

Visking tubing containing sugar solution

pure water

The water <u>rises up the tube</u> because water <u>enters</u> through the visking tubing by <u>osmosis</u>. The <u>glucose</u> molecules are <u>too big</u> to diffuse <u>out</u> into the water.

Learn The facts about Osmosis...

Osmosis can be kind of confusing if you don't get to the bottom of it. In normal diffusion, glucose molecules move, but with small enough holes they can't. That's when only water moves through the membrane, and then it's called <u>osmosis</u>. Easy peasy, I'd say. <u>Learn and enjoy</u>.

Growth Hormones in Plants

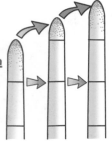

Auxins are Plant Growth Hormones

1) Auxins are hormones which control growth at the tips of shoots and roots.

2) Auxin is produced in the tips and diffuses backwards to stimulate the cell elongation process which occurs in the cells just behind the tips.

3) If the tip of a shoot is removed, no auxin will be available and the shoot may stop growing.

Auxins Change The Direction of Root and Shoot Growth

You'll note below that extra auxin promotes growth in the shoot but actually inhibits growth in the root — but also note that this produces the desired result in both cases.

1) Shoots bend towards the light

1) When a shoot tip is exposed to light, it provides more auxin on the side that is in the shade than the side which is in the light.

2) This causes the shoot to grow faster on the shaded side and it bends towards the light.

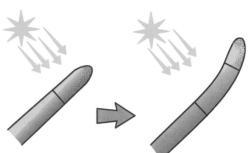

2) Shoots bend away from Gravity

1) When a shoot finds itself growing sideways, gravity produces an unequal distribution of auxin in the tip, with more auxin on the lower side.

2) This causes the lower side to grow faster, thus bending the shoot upwards.

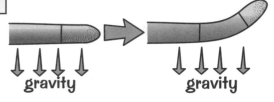
gravity   gravity

3) Roots bend towards Gravity

1) A root growing sideways will experience the same redistribution of auxin to the lower side.

2) But in a root the extra auxin actually inhibits growth, causing it to bend downwards instead.

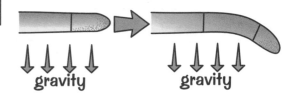
gravity   gravity

4) Roots bend towards Moisture

1) An uneven degree of moisture either side of a root will cause more auxin to appear on the side with more moisture.

2) This inhibits growth on that side, causing the root to grow in that direction, towards the moisture.

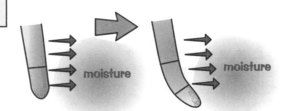
moisture   moisture

Just A Few Tips for Your Revision...

An easy page to learn. Just 3 points on auxins, together with a diagram, and then four ways that shoots and roots change direction, with a diagram for each. You just have to learn it. Then cover the page and scribble down the main points from memory. Then try again and again...

Commercial Use of Hormones

Plant hormones have a lot of uses in the <u>food growing business</u>.

1) Controlling the Ripening of Fruit

1) The <u>ripening</u> of fruits can be controlled either while they are <u>still on the plant</u>, or during <u>transport</u> to the shops.

2) This allows the fruit to be picked while it's still <u>unripe</u> (and therefore firmer and <u>less easily damaged</u>).

3) It can then be sprayed with <u>ripening hormone</u> and it will ripen <u>on the way</u> to the supermarket to be perfect just as it reaches the shelves.

2) Growing from Cuttings with Rooting Compound

1) A <u>cutting</u> is part of a plant that has been <u>cut off it</u>, like the end of a branch with a few leaves on it.

2) Normally, if you stick cuttings in the soil they <u>won't grow</u>, but if you add <u>rooting compound</u>, which is a plant <u>growth hormone</u>, they will produce roots rapidly and start growing as <u>new plants</u>.

3) This enables growers to produce lots of <u>clones</u> (exact copies) of a really good plant <u>very quickly</u>.

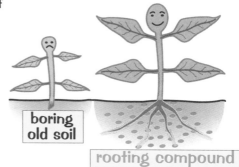

boring old soil

rooting compound

3) Killing Weeds

1) Most weeds growing in fields of crops or in a lawn are <u>broad-leaved</u>, in contrast to grass which has very <u>narrow leaves</u>.

2) <u>Selective weedkillers</u> have been developed from <u>plant growth hormones</u> which only affects the broad-leaved plants.

3) They totally <u>disrupt</u> their normal <u>growth patterns</u>, which soon <u>kills</u> them, whilst leaving the grass untouched.

Unhappy weeds

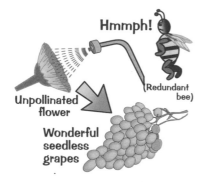

Hmmph!

(Redundant bee)

Unpollinated flower

Wonderful seedless grapes

4) Producing Seedless Fruit

You can use hormones to produce seedless satsumas and seedless grapes which are just <u>so much nicer</u> than those 'natural' ones full of pips.

Remember, serious learning always bears fruit...

Another blissfully easy page. Just make sure you learn enough about each bit to answer a 3 mark Exam question on it (that means being able to make 3 valid points). As usual the sections are split into numbered points to help you remember them. They've all got three points to learn. <u>So learn them</u>. Then <u>cover the page</u> and <u>scribble down</u> the 3 points for each . And tell me this: — if you can't do it now, what makes you think it'll all suddenly *'come back to you'* in the Exam?

The Eye

Learn The Eye with all its labels:

1) The tough outer <u>sclera</u> has a transparent region at the front called the <u>cornea</u>.

2) The <u>pupil</u> is the <u>hole</u> in the middle of the <u>iris</u>, which the <u>light goes through</u>.

3) The size of the pupil is controlled by the <u>muscular</u> iris.

4) The lens is held in position by <u>suspensory ligaments</u> and <u>ciliary muscles</u>.

5) The <u>retina</u> is the <u>light sensitive</u> part and is covered in <u>receptor cells</u>. The cornea and lens produce an image on the retina.

6) Receptor cells send impulses to the brain along neurons in the <u>optic nerve</u>.

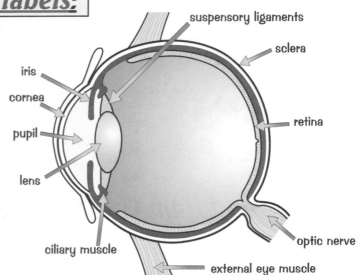

Adjusting for Light and Dark — the IRIS

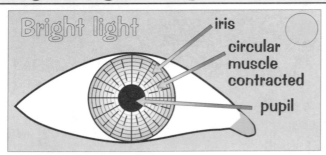

1) The circular muscles <u>contract</u>.
2) The iris <u>closes up</u>, the pupil gets <u>smaller</u>.
3) <u>Less</u> light gets into the eye.

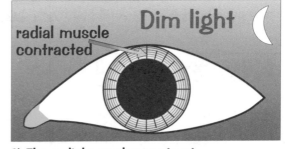

1) The radial muscles <u>contract</u>.
2) The iris <u>opens out</u>, the pupil gets <u>bigger</u>.
3) This lets <u>more light</u> into the eye.

Focusing on Near and Distant Objects

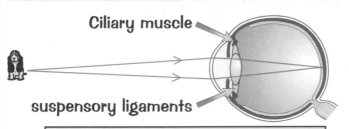

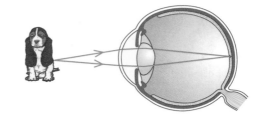

To look at <u>DISTANT objects</u>:
1) The <u>ciliary muscles relax</u>, which allows the <u>suspensory ligaments</u> to <u>pull tight</u>.
2) This makes the lens go <u>thin</u>.

To look at <u>NEAR objects</u>:
1) The <u>ciliary muscles contract</u> which <u>slackens</u> the <u>suspensory ligaments</u>.
2) The lens becomes <u>fat</u>.

Let's See What You've Learned Then...

This is a straightforward page of information. Make sure you know the diagrams with all labels and also the points for each. Practise until you can <u>scribble</u> the whole lot down <u>from memory</u>.

The Nervous System

Sense Organs and Receptors

The five sense organs are:
Eyes ears nose tongue skin

These five different sense organs all contain different receptors.

Receptors are groups of cells which are sensitive to a stimulus such as light or heat, etc.

Sense organs and Receptors
Don't get them mixed up:

The eye is a sense organ — it contains light receptors.
The ear is a sense organ — it contains sound-receptors.

Receptors are cells which change energy (eg: light energy) into electrical impulses.

The Five Sense Organs and the stimuli that each one is sensitive to:

1) Eyes
Light receptors.

2) Ears
Sound and 'balance' receptors.

3) Nose
Taste and smell receptors (Chemical stimuli).

4) Tongue
Taste receptors:
Bitter, salt, sweet and sour (Chemical stimuli).

5) Skin
Touch, pressure and temperature change.

Sensory Neurone
The nerve fibres that carry signals as electrical impulses from the receptors in the sense organs to the central nervous system.

Motor Neurone
The nerve fibres that carry signals to the effector muscle or gland.

Effectors
All your muscles and glands will respond to nervous impulses...

The Central Nervous System

1) The central nervous system is where all the sensory information is sent and where reflexes and actions are coordinated. It consists of the brain and spinal cord only.
2) Neurones (nerve cells) transmit electrical impulses very quickly around the body.
3) The effectors are muscles and glands which respond to the various stimuli according to the instructions sent from the central nervous system.

Reflex Actions Are Very Quick Automatic Responses

1) The nervous system allows very quick responses because it uses electrical impulses.
2) Reflex actions are automatic (i.e. done without thinking) so they are even quicker.
3) Reflex actions save your body from injury, eg: pulling your hand off a hot object for you.
4) A muscle responds by contracting, a gland responds by secreting.

This stuff is easy — I mean it's all just common senses...

There's quite a few names to learn here (as ever!).
But there's no drivel. It's all worth marks in the Exam, so learn it all.
Practise until you can cover the page and scribble down all the details from memory.

Homeostasis

<u>Homeostasis</u> is a fancy word. It covers lot of things, so I guess it has to be. Homeostasis covers all the functions of your body which try to maintain a <u>'constant internal environment'</u>. Learn the definition:

HOMEOSTASIS – the maintenance of a CONSTANT INTERNAL ENVIRONMENT

There are <u>six different bodily levels</u> that need to be controlled:

1) REMOVAL OF CO_2
2) REMOVAL OF <u>Urea</u>
3) <u>Ion</u> content
4) <u>Water</u> content
5) <u>Sugar</u> content
6) <u>Temperature</u>

⟸ These two are <u>wastes</u>. They're constantly produced in the body and <u>you just need to get rid of them</u>.

⟸ These four are all <u>'goodies'</u> and we need them, <u>but at just the right level</u> — not too much and not too little.

Learn the Organs Involved in Homeostasis:

The Brain

1) Contains receptors to monitor <u>blood temperature</u> and <u>water content</u> and then sends <u>nerve impulses</u> to the <u>skin</u> and to the <u>pituitary gland</u>.
2) It also <u>monitors CO_2</u> levels.

The Lungs

These <u>remove CO_2</u> and some of the <u>excess water</u>.

The Kidneys

<u>Remove urea</u>. They also adjust the <u>ion</u> and <u>water content</u> of the blood.

The Bladder

This is where <u>urine</u> is stored before departure.

Pituitary Gland

Produces many vital hormones, including <u>ADH</u>, for controlling <u>water content</u>.

The Skin

This <u>removes water</u> through <u>sweat</u> and adjusts the <u>body temperature</u>, with the help of...

The Muscles

which can produce <u>heat</u> if necessary (by <u>shivering</u>).

The Liver
The Pancreas

These two <u>work together</u> to adjust <u>blood sugar level</u>.

Controlling Our Body Temperature

All <u>enzymes</u> work best at a certain temperature. The enzymes within the human body work best at about <u>37°C</u>.

When you're too <u>cold</u> your body <u>shivers</u> (increasing your metabolism) to produce heat.

When you're too <u>hot</u> you produce <u>sweat</u> which cools you down.

Learn about Homeostasis — and keep your cool...

This is all a bit technical. Homeostasis is really quite a complicated business. It's just a good job it does it automatically or we'd all be in real trouble. You still gotta <u>learn it</u> for your Exam though. <u>Scribble</u>.

Hormones

Hormones are Chemical Messengers sent in the Blood

1) Hormones are chemicals released directly into the blood.
2) They are carried in the blood to other parts of the body.
3) They are produced in various glands (endocrine glands) as shown on the diagram.
4) They travel all over the body but only affect particular cells in particular places.
5) They travel at 'the speed of blood'.
6) They have long-lasting effects.
7) They control things that need constant adjustment.

Learn this definition:

HORMONES ...
are chemical messengers which travel in the blood to activate target cells.

The Pituitary Gland

This produces many important hormones. These tend to control other glands, as a rule.

Adrenal Gland

Produces adrenaline which prepares the body with the well known fight or flight reaction:

Increased blood sugar, heart rate, breathing rate, and diversion of blood from skin to muscles.

Pancreas

Produces insulin and glucagon for the control of blood sugar.

Kidney

Ovaries — females only
Produce oestrogen.

Testes — males only
Produce testosterone.

Hormones and Nerves do Similar Jobs, but there are Important Differences

Nerves:
1) Very fast message.
2) Act for a very short time.
3) Act on a very precise area.
4) Immediate reaction.

Hormones:
1) Slower message.
2) Act for a long time.
3) Act in a more general way.
4) Longer-term reaction.

Diabetes — the Pancreas Stops Making Enough Insulin

1) Diabetes is a disease in which the pancreas doesn't produce enough insulin.
2) The result is that a person's blood sugar can rise to a level that can kill them.
3) The problem can be controlled in two ways:

   A) A CAREFUL DIET, avoiding foods rich in carbohydrate (which turns to glucose when digested).

   B) INJECTING INSULIN into the blood before meals (especially if high in carbohydrates). This will make the liver remove the glucose from the blood as soon as it enters it from the gut, when the (carbohydrate-rich) food is being digested. This stops the level of glucose in the blood from getting too high and is a very effective treatment.

Hormones — Easy peasy...

The definition of hormones is worth learning word for word. The seven points at the top of the page and the stuff about diabetes are best done with the good old 'mini-essay' method.
Learn it, cover the page and scribble. Then try again.

Drugs

Solvents

1) Solvents are found in a variety of "household" items e.g. glues, paints etc.
2) They are <u>dangerous</u> and have many <u>damaging effects</u> on your body and personality.
3) They cause hallucinations and adversely affect personality and behaviour.
4) They cause <u>damage</u> to the <u>lungs</u>, <u>brain</u>, <u>liver</u> and <u>kidney</u>.

Alcohol

1) The main effect of alcohol is to reduce the activity of the nervous system. The positive aspect of this is that it makes us feel less inhibited, and there's no doubt that alcohol in moderation helps people to socialise and relax with each other.
2) However, if you let alcohol take over, <u>it can wreck your life</u>. And it does. It wrecks a lot of people's lives.
3) Once alcohol starts to take over someone's life there are many <u>harmful effects</u>:
   a) Alcohol is basically <u>poisonous</u>. Too much drinking will cause <u>severe damage</u> to the <u>liver</u> and the <u>brain</u> leading to <u>liver disease</u> and a noticeable <u>drop</u> in brain function.
   b) Too much alcohol <u>impairs judgement</u> which can cause accidents, and it can also severely affect the person's work and home life.
   c) Serious dependency on alcohol will eventually lead to <u>loss of job</u>, <u>loss of income</u> and the start of a <u>severe downward spiral</u>.

Smoking Tobacco

Smoking is no good to anyone except the cigarette companies.
And once you've started smoking <u>there's no going back</u>. It's a one way trip pal.

And you'll notice that smokers are <u>no happier</u> than non-smokers, <u>even when they're smoking</u>. What may start off as something "different" to do, rapidly becomes something they <u>have</u> to do, just to feel OK. But non-smokers feel just as OK <u>without</u> spending £20 or more each week and <u>wrecking their health</u> into the bargain.

And why do people start smoking? To look the part, that's why. They have an image in their head of how they want to appear and smoking seems the perfect <u>fashion accessory</u>.

Well just remember, <u>it's a one way trip</u>. You might think it makes you look cool at 16, but will it still seem the perfect fashion accessory when you're 20 with a new group of friends who don't smoke? Nope. Too late. You're stuck with it.

And by the time you're 60 it'll have cost you over £40,000. Enough to buy a Ferrari or a new house. That's quite an expensive fashion accessory. Smoking? Cool? Oh yeah — it's about as cool as cool can be, I'd say.

Oh and by the way...

Tobacco smoke does this inside your body:
1) It <u>coats</u> the <u>inside of your lungs</u> with tar so they become <u>hideously inefficient</u>.
2) It covers the cilia in <u>tar</u> preventing them from getting bacteria out of your lungs.
3) It causes <u>disease</u> of the <u>heart</u> and <u>blood vessels</u>, leading to <u>heart attacks</u> and <u>strokes</u>.
4) It causes <u>lung cancer</u>. A few years back, people didn't know this for sure but, out of every <u>ten</u> lung cancer patients, <u>nine</u> of them smoke. That's a pretty obvious connection.
5) It causes <u>severe</u> loss of lung function leading to diseases like <u>emphysema</u> and <u>bronchitis</u>, in which the inside of the lungs is basically <u>wrecked</u>. People with severe bronchitis can't manage even a brisk walk, because their lungs can't get enough oxygen into the blood. It eventually <u>kills</u> over <u>20,000 people</u> in Britain every year.

Smoking stains <u>teeth yellow</u>.
Brushing doesn't really get rid of it.

6) <u>Carbon monoxide</u> in tobacco smoke stops <u>haemoglobin</u> carrying as much oxygen. In pregnant women this deprives the foetus of oxygen leading to a small baby at birth. In short, "smoking chokes your baby".
7) But this is the best bit. The effect of the nicotine is <u>negligible</u> — other than to make you <u>addicted</u> to it.
It doesn't make you high — just <u>dependent</u>. Great. Fantastic.

Learn the Numbered Points for your Exam...

It's the disease aspects they concentrate on most in the Exams. Learn the rest for a nice life.

Revision Summary for Module Two

Jeepers creepers. Well, it's a pretty short module, but it still all needs learning.
A quick way to do this is to make use of all the pictures — these are far easier to remember than just
lists and lists of facts. Once you know the pictures it's fairly simple to tag on any extra info. You'll soon
find that simply drawing the picture will help you recall the rest. So even if the question doesn't ask for a
picture it's still worth doing a quick sketch.
Same drill as usual with these questions — keep going till you know the lot.
Just remember to use pictures to help jog your memory.

1) Sketch a typical plant cell with all its labels and three specific plant cells with all their features.
2) Sketch a typical plant and label the five important parts. Explain exactly what each bit does.
3) What does photosynthesis do? Write down the word equation for photosynthesis.
4) Sketch a leaf and show the four things needed for photosynthesis.
5) What does do plants use glucose for? What does they do in the winter?
6) What are the three variable quantities which affect the rate of photosynthesis?
7) Sketch a graph for each one and explain the shape.
8) What is the definition of diffusion and why is it important for photosynthesis?
9) What is transpiration? What causes it? What benefits does it bring?
10) How do leaves help to limit transpiration? What does this mean for plants in drier climates?
11) What are the four factors which affect the rate of transpiration?
12) What is the root hair's role in transpiration? Explain the processes involved.
13) How are minerals absorbed by the roots?
14) How do young plants use water for support? What happens if the soil dries out?
15) Explain what stomata do and how they do it.
16) What are the two types of tubes in plants? Whereabouts are they found in plants?
17) List three features for both types of tube and sketch them both.
18) Give the full strict definition of osmosis. What does it do to plant and animal cells in water?
19) Give full details of the potato tubes experiment and the visking tubing experiment.
20) What are auxins? Where are they produced?
21) Name the four ways that auxins affect roots and shoots. Give full details for all four.
22) List the four commercial uses for plant hormones. Why are ripening hormones useful?
23) Explain what rooting compound is used for. How do hormonal weed killers work?
24) Sketch a diagram of an eye and add labels. Add brief details to the labelled parts.
25) Using diagrams to show how the eye adjusts to light and dark.
26) Describe how the eye focuses on near and distant objects.
27) Draw a diagram showing the main parts of the nervous system.
28) List the five sense organs and say what kind of receptors each one has.
29) What are effectors? What two things constitute the central nervous system?
30) What are reflex reactions? Why do we need them? Give one example of a reflex reaction.
31) What is the proper definition for homeostasis? What are the six bodily levels involved?
32) Draw a diagram of the body showing the eight organs involved in homeostasis.
33) Say exactly what each of these organs does to help.
34) What temperature do our bodily enzymes like?
35) Draw a diagram of the body and label the five places where hormones are produced. Give details of what each hormones does.
36) Give the proper definition of hormones. How are they different to nerves?
37) What is diabetes? Describe the two ways that it can be controlled.
38) Draw diagrams to illustrate exactly what goes on in both cases.
39) Explain the dangers of drinking alcohol. Explain why smoking is just not cool.
40) List in detail all the major health problems that result from smoking.

The Periodic Table

The Modern Periodic Table is Ace

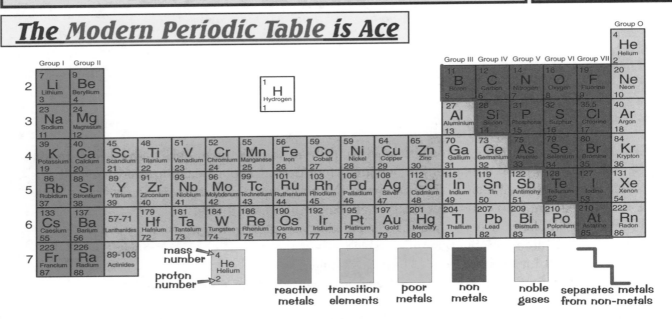

1) The Periodic Table shows the elements in order of <u>proton number</u>.
2) It's laid out so that elements with <u>similar properties</u> are in <u>columns</u>.
3) These <u>vertical columns</u> are called <u>Groups</u> and Roman Numerals are often used for them.
4) For example the <u>Group II</u> elements are Be, Mg, Ca, Sr, Ba and Ra.
   They're all <u>metals</u> which form 2+ ions and they have many other similar properties.
5) The <u>rows</u> are called <u>periods</u>. Each new period represents another <u>full shell</u> of electrons.
6) The elements in each <u>Group</u> all have the same number of <u>electrons</u> in their <u>outer shell</u>.
7) That's why they have <u>similar properties</u>. And that's why we arrange them in this way.

Argon is a bit of a Blip

1) Argon is in <u>Group 0, Period 3</u>. It has an atomic mass of <u>40</u>.
2) Potassium, which comes next in the table, has an atomic mass of <u>39</u>. If you trace your eye over the table, you'll spot that this is <u>rather curious</u> — generally, the elements get <u>heavier</u>.
3) The reason is that elements are arranged in order of <u>atomic number, Z</u>. It just happens that argon has a couple of <u>extra neutrons</u> which give it a greater <u>mass</u> than potassium, so its <u>mass number</u> is higher.

More than Three-Quarters of the Elements are Metals

<u>Three quarters</u> is a big chunk. Make sure you remember where the metals are — in the <u>two left-hand columns</u> and in the big <u>central block</u>.

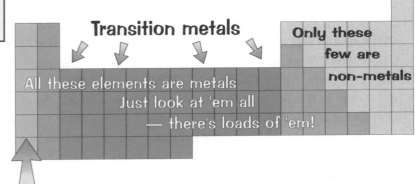

Argon is a bit of a blip, helium is a bit of a blimp...

Three quarters of all elements are metals — so it makes sense that they get a module to themselves. All this stuff comes up again in your final exam (disguised as bits of Module 8) so you're going to get <u>very familiar</u> with the Periodic Table. Mmm, lovely.

Group 1 — The Alkali Metals

You'll see this stuff again in Module 8. It's so important you have to do it twice.
They're called 'alkali metals' because their <u>hydroxides</u> dissolve in <u>water</u> to give an <u>alkaline</u> solution. Simple.

1) They are: Lithium, Sodium, Potassium and a couple more

Know those three names. They may also mention Rubidium and Caesium.

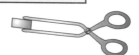

Group I

Least reactive
7 **Li** Lithium 3
23 **Na** Sodium 11
39 **K** Potassium 19
85.5 **Rb** Rubidium 37
133 **Cs** Caesium 55
223 **Fr** Francium 87
Most reactive

2) The Alkali metals are very Reactive

They have to be <u>stored in oil</u> and handled with <u>forceps</u> (they burn the skin). As you go <u>down</u> the group, they get <u>more</u> reactive.

3) The Alkali Metals are Low Density

The first three (Li, Na and K) are <u>less dense</u> than water. So they <u>float</u> on it.

4) Reaction with Cold Water produces Hydrogen Gas

1) When <u>lithium</u>, <u>sodium</u> or <u>potassium</u> are put in <u>water</u>, they react very <u>vigorously</u>.
2) They <u>move</u> around the surface, <u>fizzing</u> furiously.
3) They produce <u>hydrogen</u>. Potassium gets hot enough to <u>ignite</u> it. A lighted splint will <u>indicate</u> hydrogen by producing the notorious "<u>squeaky pop</u>" as the H_2 ignites.
4) Sodium and potassium <u>melt</u> in the heat of the reaction.
5) They form a <u>hydroxide</u> in solution, ie: <u>aqueous OH$^-$ ions</u>.

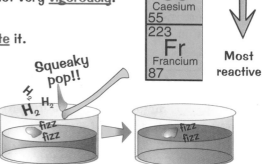

Squeaky pop!!

$$2Na_{(s)} + 2H_2O_{(l)} \rightarrow 2NaOH_{(aq)} + H_{2(g)}$$
$$2K_{(s)} + 2H_2O_{(l)} \rightarrow 2KOH_{(aq)} + H_{2(g)}$$

The solution becomes <u>alkaline</u>, which changes the colour of the pH indicator to <u>purple</u>.

5) Alkali Metal Oxides and Hydroxides are Alkaline

This means that they'll react with <u>acids</u> to form <u>neutral salts</u>, like this:

$$NaOH + HCl \rightarrow H_2O + NaCl \text{ (salt)}$$
$$Na_2O + 2HCl \rightarrow H_2O + 2NaCl \text{ (salt)}$$

6) All Alkali Compounds are Ionic and Dissolve with Glee

1) Alkali metals react with <u>non–metals</u> to form <u>ionic</u> compounds.
2) All alkali metal compounds are <u>ionic</u>, so they form <u>crystals</u> which <u>dissolve</u> in water easily to give <u>colourless</u> solutions.
3) They're all very <u>stable</u> because the alkali metals are so <u>reactive</u>.
4) Because they always form <u>ionic</u> compounds with <u>giant ionic lattices</u> the compounds all look pretty much the same, ie: <u>white crystals</u> just like regular 'salt' you put in your chip butties.

Learn about Alkali Metals — or get your fingers burnt...

Now we're getting into the seriously dreary facts section. This takes a bit of learning. <u>Enjoy</u>.

Transition Metals

Transition metals are less reactive and so do not <u>react</u> (corrode) so quickly with oxygen and water.

These are the transition metals

| | | Sc | Ti | V | 52 Cr Chromium 24 | 55 Mn Manganese 25 | 56 Fe Iron 26 | Co | 59 Ni Nickel 28 | 64 Cu Copper 29 | 65 Zn Zinc 30 | | | | | | |

Here they are, right in the middle.

1) They are Chromium, Manganese, Iron, Nickel, Copper, Zinc

You need to know the ones shown in red fairly well. If they wanted to be mean in the Exam *(if!)* they could cheerfully mention one of the others like scandium, cobalt, titanium or vanadium. Don't let it hassle you. They'll just be testing how well you can *"apply scientific knowledge to new information"*. In other words, just assume these "new" transition metals follow all the properties you've already learnt for the others. That's all it is, but it can really worry some folk.

2) Transition Metals all have high melting points and high density

They're <u>typical</u> metals. They have the properties you would expect of a proper metal:
1) <u>Good conductors</u> of heat and electricity (eg copper wire).
2) Very <u>hard</u>, <u>tough</u> and <u>strong</u>.
3) High melting points — Iron melts at 1500°C, copper melts at 1100°C and zinc melts at 400°C.
   Mercury is the exception to this rule because it is liquid at room temperature.

3) Transition Metals and their compounds make good catalysts

1) <u>Iron</u> is the catalyst used in the <u>Haber process</u> for making <u>ammonia</u>.
2) <u>Manganese (IV) oxide</u> is a good catalyst for the decomposition of <u>hydrogen peroxide</u>.
3) <u>Nickel</u> is useful for turning <u>oils into fats</u> for making margarine.

4) The compounds are very colourful

1) The compounds are colourful due to the <u>transition metal ion</u> which they contain.
   eg: Potassium chromate (VI) is <u>yellow</u>.
        Potassium manganate(VII) is <u>purple</u>.
        Copper (II) sulphate is <u>blue</u>.
2) The colour of people's <u>hair</u> and also the colours in <u>gemstones</u> like <u>blue sapphires</u> and <u>green emeralds</u> are all due to <u>transition metals</u>. <u>Weathered copper</u> is a lovely green as well. If that's not enough for you, they're also used to make <u>pottery glazes</u>.

Lots of pretty colours — that's what we like to see...

There's quite a few things to learn about transition metals. First try to remember the five headings. Then learn the details that go under each one. <u>Keep trying to scribble it all down</u>.

The Reactivity Series of Metals

You must learn this Reactivity Series

You really should know which are the more reactive metals and which are the less reactive ones.

THE REACTIVITY SERIES

POTASSIUM	K
SODIUM	Na
CALCIUM	Ca
MAGNESIUM	Mg
ALUMINIUM	Al
(CARBON)	
ZINC	Zn
IRON	Fe
LEAD	Pb
(HYDROGEN)	
COPPER	Cu
SILVER	Ag
GOLD	Au
PLATINUM	Pt

Very Reactive

Fairly Reactive

Not very Reactive

Not at all Reactive

Metals <u>above carbon</u> must be extracted from their ores by <u>electrolysis</u>.

Metals <u>below carbon</u> can be extracted from their ore using <u>reduction</u> with <u>coke or charcoal</u>.

Metals <u>below hydrogen</u> don't react with <u>water</u> or <u>acid</u>. They don't easily <u>tarnish</u> or <u>corrode</u>.

This <u>reactivity series</u> was determined by doing experiments to see how <u>strongly</u> metals <u>react</u>. The <u>three standard reactions</u> to determine reactivity are with 1) <u>air</u> 2) <u>water</u> and 3) <u>dilute acid</u>. These are <u>important</u> so make sure you know about all three in reasonable detail, as follows:

Reacting Metals in Air

1) <u>Most metals</u> will lose their <u>bright surface</u> over a period of time (they "tarnish").

2) The <u>dull</u> finish they get is due to a layer of <u>oxide</u> that forms.

3) <u>Heating them</u> makes it easier to see how <u>reactive</u> they are, compared to each other.

4) The equation is <u>real simple</u>:

layer of oxide

Reaction with Air

POTASSIUM SODIUM CALCIUM MAGNESIUM	Burn very easily with a bright flame
ALUMINIUM ZINC IRON LEAD COPPER	React slowly with air when heated
SILVER GOLD	No reaction

Metal + Oxygen → Metal Oxide

Examples: 1) $2Fe + O_2 \rightarrow 2FeO$ 2) $4Na + O_2 \rightarrow 2Na_2O$

How to get a good reaction — just smile ... ☺

Believe it or not, this should be in your brain already from KS3. But it's probably been squeezed out to make way for stuff that's more fun. That means <u>all these details need learning</u>. Again.

Reactivity of Metals

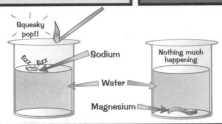

Reacting Metals With Water

1) If a metal reacts with water it will always release hydrogen.
2) The more reactive metals react with cold water to form hydroxides:

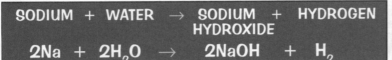

SODIUM + WATER → SODIUM HYDROGEN
HYDROXIDE

$$2Na + 2H_2O \rightarrow 2NaOH + H_2$$

3) The less reactive metals don't react quickly with water but will react with steam to form oxides:

Magnesium ribbon

Steam

Squeaky pop!!

Hydrogen?
What do ya reckon?

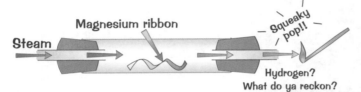

ZINC + WATER → ZINC OXIDE + HYDROGEN

$$Zn + H_2O \rightarrow ZnO + H_2$$

Reaction with Water

POTASSIUM SODIUM CALCIUM	React with cold water
MAGNESIUM ALUMINIUM ZINC	React with steam
IRON	Reacts reversibly with steam
LEAD COPPER SILVER GOLD	No reaction with water or steam

Reacting Metals With Dilute Acid

Magnesium   Aluminium   Zinc   Iron   Copper

Big squeaky pop!   Fair old squeaky pop!   Muted squeaky pop!   Squeak   No chance matey.

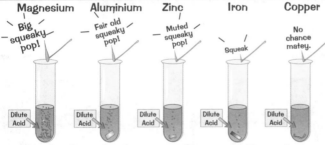

Dilute Acid   Dilute Acid   Dilute Acid   Dilute Acid   Dilute Acid

1) Metals above hydrogen in the reactivity series react with acids. Those below hydrogen won't.
2) The reaction becomes slower as you go down the series — as you'd expect.
3) The equation is real simple:

METAL + ACID → SALT + HYDROGEN

$$Mg + 2HCl \rightarrow MgCl_2 + H_2$$

Reaction with Dilute Acid

POTASSIUM SODIUM CALCIUM	Violent reaction with dilute acids
MAGNESIUM ALUMINIUM ZINC IRON	React fairly well with dilute acids
LEAD COPPER SILVER GOLD	No reaction with dilute acids

These reactions with water and acids are "Competition Reactions"

1) If the metal is more reactive than hydrogen it pushes the hydrogen out, hence the bubbles.
2) The metal replaces the hydrogen in the compound. Eg: in water, the metal "steals" the oxygen from the hydrogen to form a metal oxide. The hydrogen is then released as gas bubbles.
3) If the metal is less reactive than hydrogen, then it won't be able to displace it and nothing will happen.

All this just to say "some metals react more than others"...

I must say there's quite a lot of tricky details in these two pages. It's tempting to say that they can't possibly expect you to know them all. But then you look at the Exam questions and there they are, asking you precisely these kinds of tricky details. Tough toffee, pal. _Learn and enjoy_.

Metal Displacement Reactions

There's only one __golden rule__ here:

A _MORE reactive_ metal can _displace_ a _LESS reactive_ metal from a compound

1) This is such a simple idea, surely.
2) You know all about the reactivity series — some metals react _more strongly_ than _others_.
3) So if you put a _reactive_ metal like magnesium in a chemical solution you'd expect it to react.
4) If the chemical solution is a _dissolved metal compound_, then the reactive metal that you add will _replace_ the _less_ reactive metal in the compound.
5) The metal that's _kicked out_' will then appear as _fresh metal_ somewhere in the solution.
6) But if the metal added is _less reactive_ than the one in solution, then _no reaction_ will take place.
7) _Carbon_ and _hydrogen_ (non-metals) will also displace less reactive metals from their _oxides_.

The Virtually World Famous Iron Nail in Copper Sulphate demo

A _MORE_ REACTIVE METAL WILL _DISPLACE_ A _LESS_ REACTIVE METAL:

1) Put an _iron_ nail in a solution of _copper(II) sulphate_ and you'll see _two_ things happen:

> a) The iron nail will become coated with _copper_.
> b) The _blue_ solution will turn _colourless_.

2) This is because the iron is _more_ reactive than the copper and _displaces_ it from the solution.
3) This produces _fresh copper metal_ on the nail and a _colourless_ solution of _iron sulphate_.

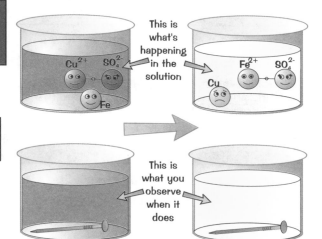

This is what's happening in the solution

This is what you observe when it does

YOU'LL ALWAYS SEE A _DEPOSIT OF METAL_ AND POSSIBLY A _COLOUR CHANGE_:

The equation is very very easy:

$$\text{iron} + \text{copper sulphate} \rightarrow \text{iron sulphate} + \text{copper}$$
$$Fe + CuSO_4 \rightarrow FeSO_4 + Cu$$

There are lots of different examples, _but they're all the same..._

Just remember the _golden rule_ at the top of the page, and you can't go wrong. The equations are always _simple_. The only tricky bit comes if the metals aren't both _2+ ions_ like in this one:

$$\text{zinc} + \text{silver nitrate} \rightarrow \text{zinc nitrate} + \text{silver}$$
$$Zn + 2AgNO_3 \rightarrow Zn(NO_3)_2 + 2Ag$$

But remember, if the metal added is _less_ reactive, nothing will happen. For example if you add _iron_ to _magnesium sulphate_ there'll be _no reaction_.

Even atoms squabble — and I thought it was only school kids...

This is simple enough. Just make sure you learn all the little details. Then cover the page and scribble down a _mini-essay_ of the main points. Then see what you missed. _Then try again._

Metal Ores from the Ground

Rocks, Minerals and Ores

1) A rock is a mixture of minerals.

2) A mineral is any solid element or compound found naturally in the Earth's crust.
Examples: Diamond (carbon), quartz (silicon dioxide), bauxite (Al_2O_3).

3) A metal ore is defined as a mineral or minerals which contain enough metal in them to make it worthwhile extracting the metal from it.

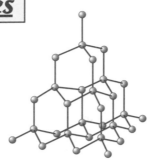

Diamond — a mineral. Each carbon atom forms four covalent bonds in a very rigid giant covalent structure.

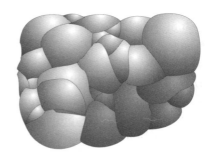

One form of iron ore, Haematite, is 90% iron and looks like this. Strange looking stuff eh?

Metals are extracted using Carbon or Electrolysis

1) Extracting a metal from its ore involves a chemical reaction to separate the metal out.

2) In many cases the metal is found as an oxide. There are three ores you need to know:

a) *Iron ore* is called *Haematite*, which is iron (III) oxide, formula Fe_2O_3.
b) *Aluminium ore* is called *Bauxite*, which is aluminium oxide, formula Al_2O_3.
c) *Copper ore* is called *Malachite*, which is copper (II) carbonate, formula $CuCO_3$.

3) The two common ways of extracting a metal from its ore are:

a) Chemical reduction using carbon or carbon monoxide eg: iron).

b) Electrolysis (breaking the ore down by passing an electric current through it).

4) Gold is one of the few metals found as a metal rather than in a chemical compound (an ore). It can be found in its pure form in rivers etc.

5) This is because gold is so unreactive.

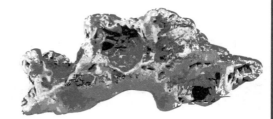

Gold Nugget

More Reactive Metals are Harder to Get

1) The more reactive metals took longer to be discovered (eg: aluminium, sodium).
2) The more reactive metals are also harder to extract from their mineral ores.
3) The above two facts are obviously related. It's obvious when you think about it...

Even primitive folk could find gold easy enough just by scrabbling about in streams, and then melt it into ingots and jewellery and statues of ABBA during their 1857 comeback tour, but coming up with a fully operational electrolysis plant to extract sodium metal from rock salt, complete with plastic yukkas in the foyer, just by paddling about a bit... unlikely.

Miners — they always have to get their ore in...

This page has three sections with lots of important points in each.
They're all important enough to need learning (except the bit about ABBA, etc.).
You need to practise repeating the details from memory. That's the only effective method.

Iron — The Blast Furnace

Iron is a <u>very common element</u> in the Earth's crust, but good iron ores are only found in <u>a few select places</u> around the world, such as Australia, Canada and Millom.

Iron is extracted from <u>haematite</u>, Fe_2O_3, by <u>reduction</u> (ie: removal of oxygen) in a <u>blast furnace</u>.

You really do need to know all these details about what goes on in a blast furnace, <u>including the equations</u>.

The Raw Materials are <u>Iron Ore, Coke</u> and <u>Limestone</u>

1) The iron ore (haematite) contains the <u>iron</u> which is pretty important.
2) The <u>coke</u> is almost pure <u>carbon</u>. This is for <u>reducing</u> the <u>iron oxide</u> to <u>iron metal</u>.
3) The <u>limestone</u> takes away impurities in the form of <u>slag</u>.

Reducing the <u>Iron Ore</u> to <u>Iron</u>:

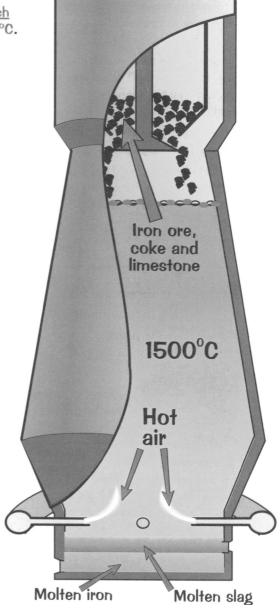

Iron ore, coke and limestone

1500°C

Hot air

Molten iron   Molten slag

1) <u>Hot air</u> is blasted into the furnace making the coke <u>burn much faster</u> than normal and the <u>temperature rises</u> to about 1500°C.

2) The <u>coke burns</u> and produces <u>carbon dioxide</u>:

$$C + O_2 \rightarrow CO_2$$
carbon + oxygen → carbon dioxide

3) The CO_2 then reacts with <u>unburnt coke</u> to form <u>CO</u>:

$$CO_2 + C \rightarrow 2CO$$
carbon dioxide + carbon → carbon monoxide

4) The <u>carbon monoxide</u> then <u>REDUCES</u> the <u>iron ore</u> to <u>iron</u>:

$$3CO + Fe_2O_3 \rightarrow 3CO_2 + 2Fe$$
carbon monoxide + iron(III)oxide → carbon dioxide + iron

The <u>carbon monoxide</u> itself combines with the <u>oxygen</u> in iron oxide to form <u>carbon dioxide</u>. This is <u>OXIDATION</u>.

5) The <u>iron</u> is of course <u>molten</u> at this temperature and it's also very <u>dense</u> so it runs straight to the <u>bottom</u> of the furnace where it's <u>tapped off</u>.

Removing the <u>Impurities</u>:

1) The <u>main impurity</u> is <u>sand</u>, (silicon dioxide). This is still <u>solid</u> even at 1500°C and would tend to stay mixed in with the iron. The limestone removes it.

2) The limestone is <u>decomposed</u> by the <u>heat</u> into <u>calcium oxide</u> and CO_2.

$$CaCO_3 \rightarrow CaO + CO_2$$

3) The <u>calcium oxide</u> then reacts with the <u>sand</u> to form <u>calcium silicate</u> or <u>slag</u> which is molten and can be tapped off:

$$CaO + SiO_2 \rightarrow CaSiO_3 \text{ (molten slag)}$$

4) The cooled slag is <u>solid</u>, and is used for:
   1) <u>Road building</u>   2) <u>Fertiliser</u>

Learn the facts about Iron Extraction — it's a blast...

Three main sections and several numbered points for each. Every bit of it is important and could be tested in the Exam, including the equations. Use the <u>mini-essay</u> method for each section. Alternatively, cover it up one section at a time, and try <u>repeating the facts</u> back to yourself. <u>And keep trying</u>.

Extracting Aluminium

A Molten State is needed for Electrolysis

1) <u>Aluminium</u> is more <u>reactive</u> than <u>carbon</u> so it has to be extracted from its ore by <u>electrolysis</u>.

2) The basic ore is <u>bauxite</u>, and after mining and purifying a white powder is left.

3) This is pure aluminium oxide, Al_2O_3, which has a <u>very high</u> melting point of over 2000°C.

4) For <u>electrolysis</u> to work a <u>molten state</u> is required, and heating to 2000°C would be <u>expensive</u>.

Cryolite is used to lower the temperature (and costs)

1) Instead, the aluminium oxide is <u>dissolved</u> in <u>molten cryolite</u> (a less common ore of aluminium).

2) This brings the temperature <u>down</u> to about 900°C, which makes it <u>much</u> cheaper and easier.

3) The <u>electrodes</u> are made of <u>graphite</u> (carbon).

4) The graphite <u>anode</u> (+ve) does need <u>replacing</u> quite often. It keeps <u>reacting</u> to form CO_2.

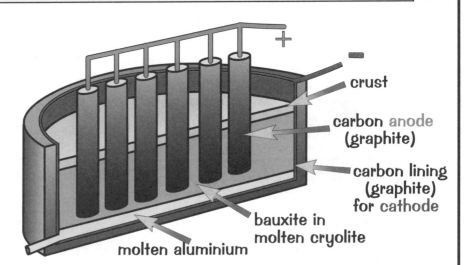

crust

carbon anode (graphite)

carbon lining (graphite) for cathode

bauxite in molten cryolite

molten aluminium

Electrolysis — turning IONS into the ATOMS you want

This is the <u>main object</u> of the exercise:

1) Make the aluminium oxide <u>molten</u> to <u>release</u> the aluminium <u>ions</u>, Al^{3+} so they're <u>free</u> to move.

2) Stick <u>electrodes</u> in — so that the <u>positive</u> Al^{3+} ions will head straight for the <u>negative electrode</u>.

3) At the negative electrode they just can't help picking up some of the <u>spare</u> <u>electrons</u> and 'zup', they've turned into aluminium <u>atoms</u> and they <u>sink to the</u> <u>bottom</u>. Pretty clever, I think.

4) The <u>aluminium</u> is drained off for casting, and the <u>oxygen</u> is separated off from the CO_2 and either used elsewhere or sold.

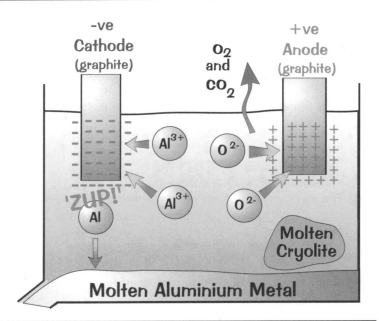

-ve Cathode (graphite)

O_2 and CO_2

+ve Anode (graphite)

Al^{3+} O^{2-}

'ZUP!'

Al^{3+} O^{2-}

Al

Molten Cryolite

Molten Aluminium Metal

Electrolysis ain't cheap — well, there's always a charge...

Four main sections with several important points to learn for each. Initially you might find it easiest to cover the sections one at a time and try to <u>recall the details</u> in your head. Ultimately though you should <u>aim to repeat it all in one go</u> with the whole page covered.

Purifying Copper by Electrolysis

1) Aluminium is a very reactive metal and has to be removed from its ore by electrolysis.

2) Copper is a very unreactive metal. Not only is it below carbon in the reactivity series, it's also below hydrogen, which means that copper doesn't even react with water.

3) So copper is obtained very easily from its ore by reduction with carbon.

Very pure copper is needed for electrical conductors

1) The copper produced by reduction isn't pure enough for use in electrical conductors.

2) The purer it is, the better it conducts. Electrolysis is used to obtain very pure copper.

3) Remember, electrolysis is not used for extracting copper from its ore $CuCO_3$ — it's simply used for further purifying copper after reduction.

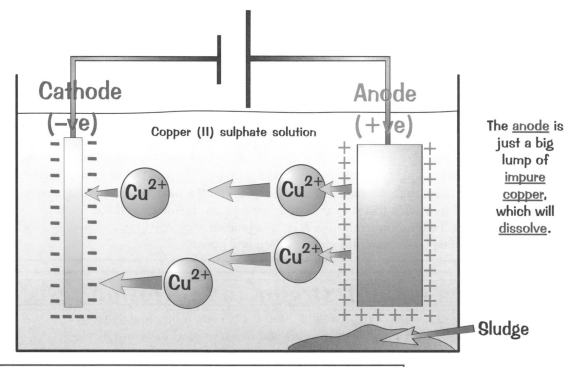

The cathode starts as a thin piece of pure copper and more pure copper adds to it.

Cathode (–ve)

Copper (II) sulphate solution

Anode (+ve)

The anode is just a big lump of impure copper, which will dissolve.

Cu^{2+}

Sludge

The Electrical Supply Controls the Electrolysis

The electrical supply acts by:

1) Pulling electrons off copper atoms at the anode causing them to go into solution as Cu^{2+} ions.

2) Then offering electrons at the cathode to nearby Cu^{2+} ions to turn them back into copper atoms.

3) The impurities are dropped at the anode as a sludge, whilst pure copper atoms bond to the cathode.

4) The electrolysis can go on for weeks and the cathode is often twenty times bigger at the end of it.

Pure copper is deposited on the pure cathode (–ve)

Copper dissolves from the impure anode (+ve)

Revision and Electrolysis — they can both go on for weeks...

This is a pretty easy page to learn. The mini-essay method will do you proud here. Don't forget the diagram and the equations. I know it's not much fun, but think how useful all this chemistry will be in your day-to-day life once you've learned it... hmmm, well... learn it anyway.

Corrosion

Corrosion is Oxidation

1) Reactive metals form oxides quite quickly when exposed to the air. This is corrosion.
2) Most metals form quite decent hard oxides that make a good protective layer.
3) A little helpful oxidation like this is a good thing but further corrosion turns more of the metal into its oxide, making it look horrid and go all crumbly.
4) Manufacturers prevent or slow down corrosion to make their metal products last longer.

Iron is Made into Steel which is Cheap and Strong

Woe of woes, iron is one metal that doesn't form a protective oxide layer. No, iron forms the most appalling red flaky oxide imaginable — the metal we use the most just had to be the one that turns to horrible useless rust. When God invented all the elements I bet he had a good old cackle to himself over that one.

IRON AND STEEL: ADVANTAGES: Cheap and strong.

DISADVANTAGES: Heavy, and prone to rusting away.

USED FOR: Bridges, buildings, cars, lorries, trains, boats and definitely NOT aeroplanes.

Bond Zinc to it or Add Chromium to Prevent Corrosion

1) Bonding a layer of zinc metal onto the surface of steel stops it rusting. The zinc soon reacts with the air to form zinc oxide which gives a good protective layer. This is called 'sacrificial protection' — any metal more reactive than iron can be used but it's mostly zinc or magnesium. Iron and steel treated in this way are used for: bridges, buildings and dustbins.
2) Mixing the steel with chromium makes an alloy called stainless steel. It doesn't oxidise so it's used for shiny cutlery and pans.

Aluminium is light, strong and corrosion-resistant

Strictly speaking you shouldn't say it's 'light', you should say it has 'low density'. Whatever. All I know is, it's a lot easier to lift and move around than iron or steel.

ADVANTAGES:
1) Lightweight. (OK, 'low density'.)
2) It's easy to bend and shape
3) It's also a good conductor of heat and electricity.
4) Doesn't corrode due to the protective layer of oxide which quickly covers it. This oxide is helpful corrosion — it forms a barrier to oxygen and water, stopping further corrosion.

DISADVANTAGES: Not as strong as steel and a bit more expensive.

USED FOR:
Ladders, aeroplanes, drink cans (tin-plated steel ones can rust if damaged), greenhouses and window frames, big power cables on pylons.

Its Alloys are Stronger and Harder

1) Mixing aluminium with other metals makes it stronger, stiffer and harder.
2) A common aluminium alloy is made by adding magnesium.

Metals are a lot more interesting than most people ever realise.*

Well, what have we here! Some chemistry which is useful in everyday life. It's pretty helpful if you know the difference between various different metals, although I guess it's only really important if you plan to build your own steam engine or rocket or something. If you don't, you'll just have to learn it for the Exam.

Acids and Alkalis

The pH Scale and Universal Indicator

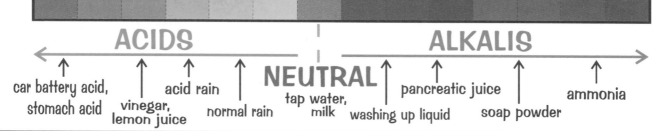

pH 1 2 3 4 5 6 7 8 9 10 11 12 13 14

ACIDS | NEUTRAL | ALKALIS

car battery acid, stomach acid — vinegar, lemon juice — acid rain — normal rain — tap water, milk — washing up liquid — pancreatic juice — soap powder — ammonia

An Indicator is just a Dye that changes colour

The dye changes colour depending on whether it's in an acid or in an alkali.
Universal indicator is a very useful combination of dyes which give the colours shown above.

The pH scale goes from 1 to 14

1) The strongest acid has pH 1.   The strongest alkali has pH 14.
2) If something is neutral it has pH 7 (eg: pure water).
3) Anything less than 7 is acid. Anything more than 7 is alkaline. (An alkali can also be called a base.)

Acids have H⁺ ions   Alkalis have OH⁻ ions

The strict definitions of acids and alkalis are:

ACIDS are substances which form $H^+_{(aq)}$ ions when added to water.

ALKALIS are substances which form $OH^-_{(aq)}$ ions when added to water.

Neutralisation

This is the equation for any neutralisation reaction.
Make sure you learn it:

acid + alkali → salt + water

Three "Real life" Examples of Neutralisation:

1) Indigestion is caused by too much hydrochloric acid in the stomach.
   Indigestion tablets contain alkalis such as magnesium oxide, which neutralise the excess HCl.

2) Fields with acidic soils can be improved no end by adding lime (See P.49).
   The lime added to fields is calcium hydroxide $Ca(OH)_2$ which is of course an alkali.

3) Lakes affected by acid rain can also be neutralised by adding lime. This saves the fish.

Hey man, like "acid", yeah — eeuuucch...

Try and enjoy this page on acids and alkalis, because it gets really tedious from now on. These are very basic facts and possibly quite interesting. Cover the page and scribble them down.

Acids Reacting With Metals

Acid + Metal → Salt + Hydrogen

That's written big 'cos it's kinda worth remembering. Here's the typical experiment:

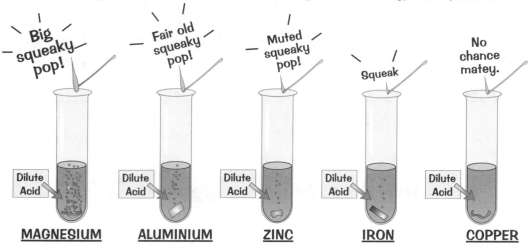

Big squeaky pop! — Fair old squeaky pop! — Muted squeaky pop! — Squeak — No chance matey.

Copper is _less reactive_ than _hydrogen_ so it doesn't react with dilute acids at all.

Dilute Acid — Dilute Acid — Dilute Acid — Dilute Acid — Dilute Acid

MAGNESIUM   **ALUMINIUM**   **ZINC**   **IRON**   **COPPER**

1) The more reactive the metal, the faster it will go.
2) Copper does not react with dilute acids at all — because it's less reactive than hydrogen.
3) The speed of reaction is indicated by the rate at which the bubbles of hydrogen are given off.
4) The hydrogen is confirmed by the burning splint test giving the notorious 'squeaky pop'.
5) The type of salt produced depends on which metal is used, and which acid is used:

Hydrochloric acid produces chloride salts:

$2HCl + Mg \rightarrow MgCl_2 + H_2$ (Magnesium chloride)

$6HCl + 2Al \rightarrow 2AlCl_3 + 3H_2$ (Aluminium chloride)

$2HCl + Zn \rightarrow ZnCl_2 + H_2$ (Zinc chloride)

Sulphuric acid produces sulphate salts:

$H_2SO_4 + Mg \rightarrow MgSO_4 + H_2$ (Magnesium sulphate)

$3H_2SO_4 + 2Al \rightarrow Al_2(SO_4)_3 + 3H_2$ (Aluminium sulphate)

$H_2SO_4 + Zn \rightarrow ZnSO_4 + H_2$ (Zinc sulphate)

Nitric acid produces nitrate salts when NEUTRALISED, but...

Nitric acid reacts fine with alkalis, to produce nitrates. But it can play silly devils with metals and produce nitrogen oxides instead, so we'll ignore it here. Chemistry's a really messy subject sometimes.

Ammonia produces ammonium salts

Ammonia dissolves in water to make an alkaline solution.
This is neutralised with acids to make ammonium salts.

Revision of Acids and Metals — easy as squeaky pop...

Actually, this stuff isn't too bad I don't think. I mean it's *fairly* interesting. Not quite in the same league as Dawson's Creek, I'll give you that, but for Chemistry it's not bad at all. At least there's bubbles and flames and noise and that kinda thing. Anyway, learn it, scribble it down, etc...

Acids with Oxides and Hydroxides

Metal Oxides and Metal Hydroxides are Alkalis

1) Metal underline(oxides) and metal underline(hydroxides) are generally underline(alkalis).

2) Oxides and hydroxides of underline(transition) metals underline(won't) dissolve in underline(water). They are called underline(BASES).

3) Other metal oxides and metal hydroxides dissolve in water to produce alkaline solutions.

4) All metal oxides and hydroxides react with acids to form a salt and water:

> ## Acid + Metal Oxide → Salt + Water

> ## Acid + Metal Hydroxide → Salt + Water

(These are neutralisation reactions of course)

The Combination of Metal and Acid decides the Salt

This isn't exactly exciting but it's pretty easy, so try and get the hang of it:

Hydrochloric acid	+	Copper oxide	→	Copper chloride	+ water
Hydrochloric acid	+	Sodium hydroxide	→	Sodium chloride	+ water
Sulphuric acid	+	Zinc oxide	→	Zinc sulphate	+ water
Sulphuric acid	+	Calcium hydroxide	→	Calcium sulphate	+ water
Nitric acid	+	Magnesium oxide	→	Magnesium nitrate	+ water
Nitric acid	+	Potassium hydroxide	→	Potassium nitrate	+ water

The symbol equations are all pretty much the same. Here's two of them:

$$H_2SO_4 + ZnO \rightarrow ZnSO_4 + H_2O$$
$$HNO_3 + KOH \rightarrow KNO_3 + H_2O$$

An Indicator shows when the Reaction is Finished

The best way to tell that you've made a neutral salt and water is to use an indicator. Otherwise you'd have to keep dunking in a sad little piece of litmus paper to test it.

Universal indicator is the best to use and it doesn't affect the reaction at all. It'll go red when you add it to the acid. Then as you add the alkali to it, it'll change to orange, yellow then green when all that's left is the salt and water.

Acids are really dull, aren't they — learn and snore...

You've gotta be a pretty serious career chemist to find this stuff interesting.
Normal people (like you and me) just have to grin and bear it. Oh, and learn it as well, of course — don't forget the small matter of those little Exams you've got coming up...

Revision Summary for Module Five

Phew, I'll you what you know — there's some serious Chemistry in this module.
I suppose it makes up for some of the other modules being so easy. This is where all the really grisly stuff is. All I can say is, just keep trying to learn it. These jolly questions will give you some idea of how well you're doing. For any you can't do, you'll find the answers somewhere in Module Five.

1) What proportion of the elements are metals? Why is argon an oddity?
2) Write down the twelve common metals in the order of the Reactivity Series.
3) Where do carbon and hydrogen fit in and what is the significance of their positions?
4) Describe the reaction of all twelve metals when heated in air. (Yes, *twelve*)
5) What is the word equation for a metal reacting with oxygen?
6) Describe the reaction of all twelve metals with water (or steam).
7) Describe the reaction of all twelve metals with dilute acid.
8) What type of reaction is this? Give two examples, with equations.
9) What is the 'golden rule' of metal displacement reactions?
10) What are the tell-tale signs that a metal displacement reaction has taken place?
11) A lead weight is put into a beaker containing zinc nitrate. What happens?
12) An iron beaker is filled with silver nitrate. What happens?
13) What are rocks, ores and minerals? Name a metal is found as itself rather than an ore.
14) Give the chemical formulae of these three ores: iron ore, aluminium ore and copper ore.
15) What are the two methods for extracting metals from their ores?
16) What property of the metal decides which method is needed?
17) Draw a diagram of a blast furnace. What are the three raw materials used in it?
18) Write down the equations for how iron is obtained from its ore in the blast furnace.
19) How are the impurities removed from the iron? Give equations.
20) How is aluminium extracted from its ore? Give four operational details and draw a diagram.
21) Write down the redox equations for how aluminium is obtained from its ore.
22) Explain why the electrolysis of aluminium is so expensive.
23) How is copper extracted from its ore?
24) How is copper then purified, and why does it need to be?
25) Draw a diagram for the purifying process.
26) Where is the pure copper obtained?
27) What is corrosion?
28) Describe the plus and minus points of iron (and steel), and give four uses for it.
29) Describe two methods used to stop iron and steel rusting.
30) Describe the plus and minus points of aluminium, and give four uses for it.
31) How can aluminium be made stronger and harder?
32) Describe fully the colour of universal indicator for every pH value from 1 to 14.
33) What type of ions are always present in a) acids and b) alkalis? What is neutralisation?
34) What is the equation for reacting acid with metal? Which metal(s) don't react with acid?
35) Give three real-life examples of the practical benefits of neutralising acids and alkalis.
36) To what extent do Cu, Al, Mg, Fe and Zn react with dilute acid? What would you see?
37) When a burning splint is held over the test tubes, how loud would the different squeaky pops be?
38) What type of salts do hydrochloric acid and sulphuric acid produce?
39) What type of reaction is "acid + metal oxide", or "acid + metal hydroxide"?

Four Uses Of Limestone

Limestone

Limestone is a sedimentary rock, formed mainly from sea shells. It is mostly calcium carbonate.

1) Limestone Used as a Building Material

1) It's great for making into blocks for building with.
   Fine old buildings like cathedrals are often made purely
   from limestone blocks. Acid rain can be a problem though.
2) For statues and fancy carved bits on nice buildings.
   But acid rain is even more of a problem.
3) It can just be crushed up into chippings and
   used for road surfacing.

2) Limestone for Neutralising Acid in lakes and soil

1) Ordinary limestone ground into powder can be used to neutralise acidity in lakes
   caused by acid rain. It can also be used to neutralise acid soils in fields.
2) It works better and faster if it's turned into slaked lime first:

Turning Limestone into Slaked Lime: first heat it up, then add water

1) The limestone is heated and it turns into calcium oxide (CaO) and carbon dioxide.

$$limestone \xrightarrow{HEAT} quicklime$$ or $$CaCO_3 \xrightarrow{HEAT} CaO + CO_2$$

2) This reaction is a *thermal decomposition*.
3) Calcium oxide reacts violently with water to produce calcium hydroxide (or slaked lime):

$$quicklime + water \longrightarrow slaked\ lime$$ or $$CaO + H_2O \longrightarrow Ca(OH)_2$$

4) Slaked lime is a white powder and can be applied to fields just like powdered limestone.
5) The advantage is that slaked lime acts much faster at reducing the acidity.

3) Limestone and Clay are Heated to Make Cement

1) Clay contains aluminium and silicates and is dug out of the ground.
2) Powdered clay and powdered limestone are roasted in a rotating kiln to produce a complex mixture
   of calcium and aluminium silicates, called cement.
3) When cement is mixed with water a slow chemical reaction takes place.
4) This causes the cement to gradually set hard.
5) Cement is usually mixed with sand and chippings to make concrete.
6) Concrete is a very quick and cheap way of constructing buildings — and it shows...
   — concrete has got to be the most hideously unattractive building material ever known.

4) Glass is made by melting Limestone, Sand and Soda

1) Just heat up limestone (calcium carbonate)
   with sand (silicon dioxide) and soda
   (sodium carbonate) until it melts.
2) When the mixture cools it comes out as glass.
   It's as easy as that. Eat your heart out, Mr. Pilkington.

Tough Revision here — this stuff's rock hard...

I bet when those little sea creatures died all those millions of years ago, they had no idea they would one
day become the cornerstones of 20th century civilisation. Get it! — *cornerstones.* Chortle chortle.
Anyway, enough frivolity. Learn the whole page till you've got it *rock solid...*

Crude Oil

Fossil Fuels were formed from dead plants and animals

1) <u>Fossil fuels</u> have formed over <u>millions</u> of years.

2) Plants and animals <u>died</u> and were <u>immediately</u> covered by <u>sediment</u> in <u>seas</u> or <u>swamps</u>.

3) This <u>stopped</u> them decaying.

4) Further layers of sediment buried the plant and animal remains <u>deeper</u> and <u>deeper</u>.

5) After <u>millions</u> of years of <u>pressure and heat</u> (90°C to 120°C), in an environment with no air, these remains turned into <u>coal</u>, <u>oil</u> and <u>natural gas</u>.

6) When we burn fossil fuels we're using the <u>sun's energy</u> that has been stored as <u>chemical energy</u> underground for <u>millions</u> of years.

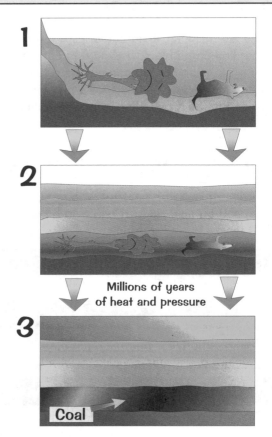

Millions of years of heat and pressure

Coal

Crude oil is a very big part of modern life

1) It provides the <u>fuel</u> for most modern transport.

2) It also provides the <u>raw material</u> for making various <u>chemicals</u> including <u>plastics</u>. Plastics are just ace, of course. The world without plastics? Why, it would be the end of civilisation as we know it...

Crude oil has to be split up to make it useful

1) <u>Crude oil</u> is a mixture of different sized <u>hydrocarbon</u> molecules.

2) <u>Hydrocarbons</u> are basically <u>fuels</u> such as petrol and diesel.

3) The <u>bigger</u> and <u>longer</u> the molecules, the <u>less runny</u> the hydrocarbon (fuel) is.

4) <u>Fractional distillation</u> splits crude oil up into its separate <u>fractions</u>.

5) The <u>shorter the molecules</u>, the <u>lower the temperature</u> at which that fraction <u>condenses</u>.

OK, so it's an easy page — don't let it go to your head...

A typical question would show a fractionating column (coming up over the page) and ask you which bit you'd expect petrol or diesel to come out of, or ask you how long the carbon chain of diesel is, or ask you to give the main uses of crude oil. So make sure you know <u>all</u> the details. When you think you do, <u>cover up the page</u> and <u>scribble down</u> all the details. <u>Then try again</u>.

Distillation of Crude Oil

Crude Oil is Split into Separate Hydrocarbons (fuels)

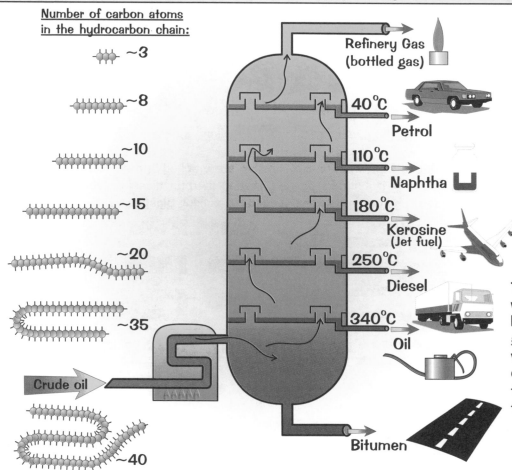

Number of carbon atoms in the hydrocarbon chain:

~3

~8

~10

~15

~20

~35

Crude oil

~40

Refinery Gas (bottled gas)

40°C — Petrol

110°C — Naphtha

180°C — Kerosine (Jet fuel)

250°C — Diesel

340°C — Oil

Bitumen

The <u>fractionating column</u> works continuously, with heated crude oil piped in <u>at the bottom</u> and the various <u>fractions</u> being constantly tapped off at the different levels where they <u>condense</u>.

Hydrocarbons are long chain molecules

As the <u>size</u> of the hydrocarbon molecule <u>increases</u>:

1) The *BOILING POINT* increases

2) It gets *LESS FLAMMABLE*
(doesn't set fire so easy)

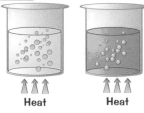

Heat   Heat

3) It gets *MORE VISCOUS*
(doesn't flow so easy)

4) It gets *LESS VOLATILE*

The <u>vapours</u> of the more <u>volatile</u> hydrocarbons are <u>very flammable</u> and pose a serious <u>fire risk</u>. So don't smoke at the petrol station. (In fact, don't smoke at all, it's stupid.)

The one burning question is... have you learnt it all...

You need to learn the four features of hydrocarbons which change with increasing chain length. All worth <u>juicy marks</u> in the Exam. So learn and enjoy.

Cracking Hydrocarbons

Cracking — splitting up long chain hydrocarbons

1) <u>Long chain</u> hydrocarbons form <u>thick</u> gloopy liquids like <u>tar</u> which aren't all that useful.
2) The process called <u>cracking</u> turns them into <u>shorter</u> molecules which are <u>much</u> more useful.

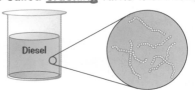 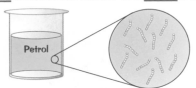

3) <u>Cracking</u> is a form of <u>thermal decomposition</u>, which just means <u>breaking</u> molecules down into <u>simpler</u> molecules by <u>heating</u> them.
4) A lot of the longer molecules produced from fractional distillation are <u>cracked</u> into smaller ones because there's <u>more demand</u> for products like <u>petrol</u> and <u>kerosene</u> (jet fuel) than for diesel or lubricating oil.
5) More importantly, cracking produces <u>chemicals</u> that are needed for making <u>plastics</u>.

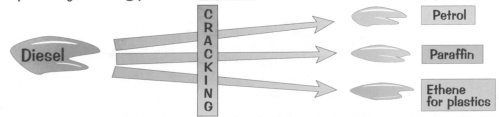

Industrial Conditions for Cracking: hot, plus a catalyst

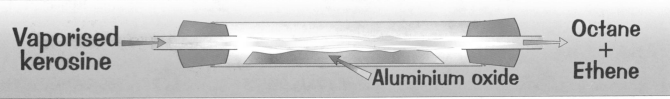

1) <u>Vaporised hydrocarbons</u> are passed over a <u>powdered catalyst</u> at about <u>400°C – 700°C</u>.
2) <u>Aluminium oxide</u> is the catalyst used.
   The <u>long chain</u> molecules <u>split apart</u> or "crack" on the <u>surface</u> of the bits of catalyst.
   This is another of those <u>thermal decomposition</u> reactions.

There are loads of Plastics with loads of different uses

1) Polythene

1) Made from <u>ethene</u>
2) Very <u>cheap</u> and <u>strong</u>
3) Easily <u>moulded</u>

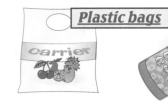  

2) Polypropene

1) Made from <u>propene</u>.
2) Forms <u>strong fibres</u>
3) Has <u>high elasticity</u>

Chemistry — what a cracking subject it is...

Five details about the whys and wherefores, two details of the industrial conditions and some examples of stuff you can make with plastics. Rivetting stuff, but you've got to <u>LEARN IT ALL</u>.

Gases in the Atmosphere

The Earth's atmosphere wasn't always as it is today. Here's how the first 4.5 billion years have gone:

Phase 1 — Volcanoes gave out Steam, CO_2, NH_3 and CH_4

The First Billion Years

1) The Earth's surface was originally molten for many millions of years. Any atmosphere boiled away.

2) Eventually it cooled and a thin crust formed but volcanoes kept erupting, releasing mainly carbon dioxide.

3) But also some steam, ammonia and methane.

4) The early atmosphere was mostly CO_2 (virtually no oxygen).

5) The water vapour condensed to form the oceans.

Phase 2 — Green Plants Evolved and produced Oxygen

1) Green plants evolved over most of the Earth.

2) A lot of the early CO_2 dissolved into the oceans.

3) But the green plants steadily removed CO_2 and produced O_2.

4) Much of the CO_2 from the air thus became locked up in fossil fuels and sedimentary rocks.

5) Methane and ammonia reacted with the oxygen, releasing nitrogen gas.

The Next Two Billion Years

Composition of Today's Atmosphere

The atmosphere we have today is *just right*. It has *gradually* evolved over billions of years and *we* have evolved with it. All very slowly.

(In the table, the percentages come to a bit over 100% because the first three are rounded up very slightly.)

78%	Nitrogen	(Often written as 79% Nitrogen for simplicity.)
1%	Argon	
21%	Oxygen	
0.04%	Carbon dioxide	

Also :
1) Varying amounts of *WATER VAPOUR*.
2) And other *noble gases* in very small amounts.

Burning fuels releases CO_2, water and sulphur dioxide

1) When fossil fuels are burned they release mostly CO_2.

2) Water vapour is released too — it's an oxide of the hydrogen in the fuel.

2) But they also release two other harmful gases, sulphur dioxide and various nitrogen oxides.

3) The sulphur dioxide, SO_2, comes from sulphur impurities in the fossil fuels.

Phew — is it hot in here or is it Global Warming...

It's surprising just how much stuff there is on carbon dioxide and the atmosphere, but I'm afraid there's plenty of past exam questions which ask precisely these details. If you want those marks, you've gotta learn these drivelly facts, and that's that. You know the drill: learn, cover, scribble, check... learn...

 54

The Three Different Types of Rocks

This should all be revision — there are <u>three</u> different types: <u>sedimentary</u>, <u>metamorphic</u> and <u>igneous</u>. Over <u>millions</u> of years they <u>change</u> from one into another. This is called the <u>Rock Cycle</u>. Astonishingly.

The Rock Cycle

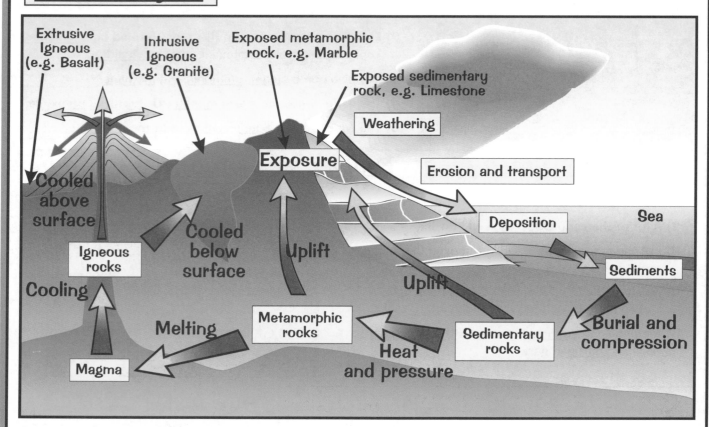

The Rocks *Change from One to Another in a Slow Cycle*

1) Particles get washed to the <u>sea</u> and settle as <u>sediment</u>.

2) Over <u>millions</u> of years these sediments get <u>crushed</u> into <u>sedimentary rocks</u> (hence the name).

3) At first they get <u>buried</u>, but they can either <u>rise</u> to the surface again to be discovered, or they can <u>descend</u> into the <u>heat</u> and <u>pressure</u> below.

4) If they <u>do</u>, the heat and pressure completely <u>alter</u> the structure of the rock and they then become <u>metamorphic rocks</u> (as in "metamorphosis" or "change". Another good name!).

5) These <u>metamorphic rocks</u> can either rise to the <u>surface</u> to be discovered by an enthusiastic geologist or else descend still <u>further</u> into the fiery abyss of the Earth's raging inferno where they will <u>melt</u> and become <u>magma</u>.

6) When <u>magma</u> reaches the surface it <u>cools</u> and <u>sets</u> and is then called <u>igneous rock</u>.
   ("igneous" as in "ignite" or "fire" — another cool name. Gee, if only biology names were this sensible.)

7) When any of these rocks reach the <u>surface</u>, then <u>weathering</u> begins and they gradually get <u>worn down</u> and carried off to the <u>sea</u> and the whole cycle starts over <u>again</u>... Simple, innit?

Rocks are a mystery — no, no, it's sedimentary my Dear Watson...

Don't you think the Rock Cycle is pretty ace? Can you think of anything you'd rather do than go on a family holiday to Cornwall, gazing at the cliffs and marvelling at the different types of rocks and stuff? Exactly. (And even if you can, it's still a good plan to <u>learn about rocks</u>.)

Evidence in Rocks

Layers One on Top of the Other = Sedimentary

1) <u>Sedimentary rocks</u> are formed from <u>layers</u> of sediment deposited in <u>lakes</u> or <u>seas</u>.
2) <u>Sandstone</u> and <u>limestone</u> are sedimentary rocks.
3) Over <u>millions of years</u> the layers get buried under more layers and the <u>weight</u> pressing down <u>squeezes</u> out the water. As the water disappears, <u>salts</u> crystallize out and <u>cement</u> the particles together.

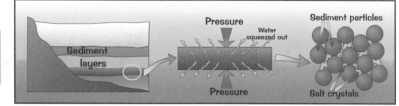

Fossils are only found in Sedimentary Rocks

1) Only <u>sedimentary</u> rocks contain <u>fossils</u>.
2) Fossils are a very useful way of <u>identifying rocks</u> as being of the <u>same age</u>.
3) This is because fossilised remains that are found <u>change</u> (due to evolution) as the <u>ages pass</u>.
4) This means that if two rocks have the <u>same fossils in</u> they must be from the <u>same age</u>.

Sediments Contain Evidence of how they were Laid Down

They contain <u>evidence</u> which tells geologists <u>how</u> the sediment was laid down. This could be:
1) <u>RIPPLE MARKS</u> — formed by currents or waves, like you see in sand when the tide's out.
2) <u>DISCONTINUOUS DEPOSITION</u> — this is when there's a gap in the fossil record (see Module 4). A layer can be eroded (eg: if the water level drops) so when next layer turns to rock, there's a <u>layer missing</u>.
3) <u>SIZE OF PARTICLES</u> — smaller particles take longer to settle to the bottom of the lake or sea so <u>mud</u>, <u>clay</u> or <u>slate</u> tells you the water was <u>quiet</u>. Bigger stuff like <u>pebbles</u> embedded in the sandstone was dumped by <u>fast flowing</u> water (eg: a river) when it got to the sea or lake.

The rock layers are often found all lining up nicely but just as often, they're found:
1) <u>TILTED</u> 2) <u>FOLDED UP</u> 3) <u>FRACTURED</u> ('<u>FAULTED</u>') 4) Turned completely <u>UPSIDE DOWN</u> (blimey).
The layers show that the Earth's crust is <u>unstable</u> and there have been <u>very large forces</u> acting on it.

Action of Heat and Pressure = Metamorphic

1) Earth movements can push all types of rocks deep underground.
2) Here they are compressed and heated and the <u>mineral structure</u> and <u>texture</u> may change over thousands of years.
3) As long as they don't actually <u>melt</u>, these changed rocks are classed as <u>metamorphic</u>.
4) The Earth shifting itself about creates mountain belts. Metamorphic rocks are the <u>evidence</u> of the <u>high temperatures</u> and <u>pressures</u> created when mountains were made.
5) New mountain ranges are created over <u>millions</u> of years. They replace ancient mountain ranges which are eventually worn down by <u>weathering</u> and <u>erosion</u>.

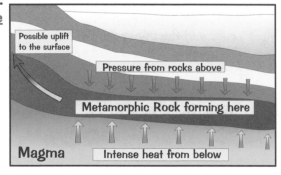

Mountain Ranges form when the Crust Moves

1) <u>Large scale</u> movements of the Earth's crust push the rocks up to form <u>mountains</u>.
2) It's incredibly <u>slow</u> — it takes <u>millions of years</u>.
3) As new mountain ranges form, they are <u>replacing</u> older ranges which are worn down by <u>erosion</u> and <u>weathering</u>.

Learn about Crusts — it'll make your hair curl...

Pretty soon you won't be able to go to the beach without playing a fun game of 'Spot the Rock Types'. Lots to learn but it's straightforward stuff. Use the titles of the sections to do mini-essays.

The Earth's Structure

Crust, Mantle, Outer and Inner Core

1) The crust is very thin (well, about 20km or so!).
2) The mantle has the properties of a solid but it can flow very slowly.
3) The core is just over half the Earth's radius.
4) The core is made from iron and nickel. This is where the Earth's magnetic field originates.
5) The iron and nickel sank to the "bottom" long ago (i.e. the centre of the Earth) because they're denser.
6) The core has a solid inner bit and a liquid outer bit.
7) Radioactive decay creates all the heat inside the Earth.
8) This heat causes the convection currents which cause the plates of the crust to move.

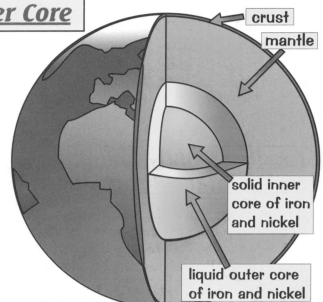

crust
mantle
solid inner core of iron and nickel
liquid outer core of iron and nickel

Big Clues: Seismic Waves, Magnetism and Meteorites

1) The overall density of the Earth is much higher than the density of rock. This means the inside must be made of something denser than rock.
2) Meteorites which crash to Earth are often made of iron and nickel.
3) Iron and nickel are both magnetic and very dense.
4) So if the core of the Earth were made of iron and nickel it would explain a lot, ie: the high density of the Earth and the fact that it has a magnetic field round it (see Module 10).
5) Also, by following the paths of seismic waves from earthquakes as they travel through the Earth, we can tell that there is a change to liquid about halfway through the Earth.
6) Hence we deduce a liquid outer core of iron and nickel. The seismic waves also indicate a solid inner core (refer to the Final Exam book). See how very easy it all is when you know.

The Earth's Surface is made up of Large Plates of Rock

1) The Earth's lithosphere is the crust and the upper part of the mantle. It's cracked into pieces called plates.

2) These plates are like big rafts that float across the liquid mantle.

3) The map shows the edges of these plates. As they move, the continents move too.

4) The plates are moving at a speed of about 1cm or 2cm per year.

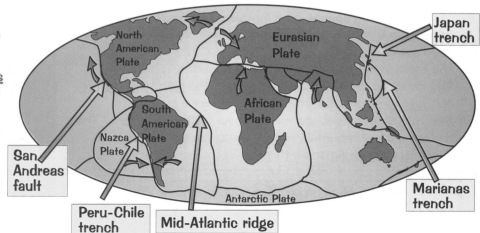

North American Plate, Eurasian Plate, Japan trench, African Plate, South American Plate, Nazca Plate, San Andreas fault, Peru-Chile trench, Mid-Atlantic ridge, Antarctic Plate, Marianas trench

Try Telling that lot to the Spanish Inquisition...

More nice easy stuff. That means it's nice easy marks in the Exam too. They do put easy stuff in, just so that everyone gets at least some marks. Just make sure you learn all the details. There's nothing dafter than missing easy marks. Cover the page and check you know it all.

Evidence for Plate Tectonics

Crinkly bits from Cooling? — I don't think so, matey

The old theory was that all the <u>features</u> of the Earth's surface, e.g. mountains, were due to <u>shrinkage</u> of the crust as it <u>cooled</u>. In the Exam they may well ask you about that, and then they'll ask you for <u>evidence</u> in favour of <u>plate tectonics</u> as a <u>better theory</u>. Learn and prosper:

1) Jigsaw Fit — the supercontinent "Pangaea"

a) There's a very obvious <u>jigsaw fit</u> between <u>Africa</u> and <u>South America</u>.

b) The <u>other</u> continents can also be fitted in without too much trouble.

c) It's widely believed that they once all formed a <u>single</u> land mass, now called <u>Pangaea</u>.

2) Matching Fossils in Africa and South America

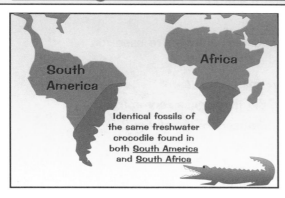

Identical fossils of the same freshwater crocodile found in both <u>South America</u> and <u>South Africa</u>

a) Identical <u>plant fossils</u> of the <u>same age</u> have been found in rocks in <u>South Africa</u>, <u>Australia</u>, <u>Antarctica</u>, <u>India</u> and <u>South America</u>, which strongly suggests they were all <u>joined</u> once upon a time.

b) <u>Animal fossils</u> support the theory too. There are identical fossils of a freshwater <u>crocodile</u> found in both <u>Brazil</u> and <u>South Africa</u>. It certainly didn't swim across.

3) Identical Rock Sequences

a) When <u>rock strata</u> of similar <u>ages</u> are studied in various countries they show remarkable <u>similarity</u>.

b) This is strong evidence that these countries were <u>joined</u> together when the rocks <u>formed</u>.

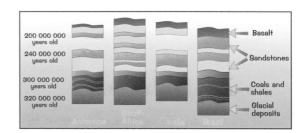

200 000 000 years old
240 000 000 years old
300 000 000 years old
320 000 000 years old

Basalt
Sandstones
Coals and shales
Glacial deposits

Antarctica   South Africa   India   Brazil

Wegener's Theory of Crustal Movement

This stuff was noticed hundreds of years ago, but nobody really believed that the continents could once have actually been joined.

In 1915, a chap called Alfred <u>Wegener</u> proposed his theory of "<u>continental drift</u>" saying that they had definitely been joined and that they were slowly drifting apart.
This wasn't accepted for two reasons:

a) he couldn't give a convincing <u>reason</u> why it happened

b) he wasn't a qualified <u>geologist</u>

Only in the 1960s with lots of <u>evidence</u> was the theory widely accepted.

Learn about Plate Tectonics — but don't get carried away...

Three bits of evidence which support the theory that there are big plates of rock moving about. Learn all three well enough to be able to answer a question like this: "Describe evidence which supports the theory of Plate Tectonics" (5 marks). <u>Learn, cover, scribble, etc...</u>

Revision Summary for Module Six

Module Six is pretty interesting stuff I reckon. Relatively speaking. Anyway, whether it is or it isn't, the only thing that really matters is whether you've learnt it all or not. These questions aren't exactly friendly, but they're a seriously serious way of finding out what you don't know. And don't forget, that's what revision is all about — finding out what you don't know and then learning it till you do. Practise these questions as often as necessary — not just once. Your ultimate aim is to be able to answer all of them easily.

1) Write down the four uses of limestone. What's slaked lime?
2) What are fossil fuels? Describe how they were formed.
3) Why is crude oil so important?
4) Draw the full diagram of fractional distillation of crude oil.
5) What are the seven main fractions obtained from crude oil, and what are they used for?
6) What are hydrocarbons? Describe four properties and how they vary with the molecule size.
7) Give a typical example of a substance which is cracked and the products that you get.
8) What are the industrial conditions used for cracking?
9) Name two types of plastic, give their physical properties and say what they're used for.
10) What does biodegradable mean?
11) How old is the Earth? What was it like for the first billion years or so?
12) What gases did the early atmosphere consist of? Where did these gases come from?
13) What was the main thing which caused phase two of the atmosphere's evolution?
14) What are the percentages of gases in today's atmosphere?
15) Which gases are produced when fossil fuels are burned?
16) What was the main thing which caused phase two of the atmosphere's evolution?
17) Which gas allowed phase three to take place?
18) What are the three types of rock? Draw a fully labelled diagram of the rock cycle.
19) Explain how the three types of rock change from one to another. How long does this take?
20) Draw diagrams to show how sedimentary rocks form.
21) What type of rock contains fossils?
22) How can fossils be used to identify rocks as being the same age?
23) What three things tell geologists how sediments were laid down?
24) As well as lining up neatly, what other four ways might you find sedimentary rock layers? What is this evidence of?
25) Draw a diagram to show how metamorphic rocks are formed. What does the name mean?
26) How are new mountain ranges formed? What happens to older mountain ranges?
27) Draw a diagram of the internal structure of the Earth, with labels.
28) What was the old theory about the Earth's surface? What is the theory of Plate Tectonics?
29) Give details of the three bits of evidence which support the theory of plate tectonics.

Energy Transfer

Learn all The Ten Types Of Energy

You should know all of these well enough to list them from memory, including the examples:

1) ELECTRICAL ENERGY.................................. — whenever a current flows.
2) LIGHT ENERGY... — from the Sun, light bulbs etc.
3) SOUND ENERGY....................................... — from loudspeakers or anything noisy.
4) KINETIC ENERGY, OR MOVEMENT ENERGY.... — anything that's moving has it.
5) NUCLEAR ENERGY.................................... — released only from nuclear reactions.
6) THERMAL ENERGY OR HEAT ENERGY............ — flows from hot objects to colder ones.
7) RADIANT HEAT ENERGY, OR INFRA RED HEAT — given out as EM radiation by hot objects.
8) GRAVITATIONAL POTENTIAL ENERGY........... — possessed by anything which can fall.
9) ELASTIC POTENTIAL ENERGY...................... — stretched springs, elastic, rubber bands, etc.
10) CHEMICAL ENERGY................................. — possessed by foods, fuels and batteries.

Potential- and Chemical- are forms of Stored Energy

The last three above are forms of stored energy because the energy is not obviously doing anything, it's kind of waiting to happen, i.e. waiting to be turned into one of the other forms.

They Like Giving Exam Questions on Energy Transfers

These are very important examples. You must learn them till you can repeat them all easily.

Eating food / respiration

Chemical → Heat / kinetic / chemical

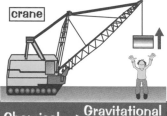
crane

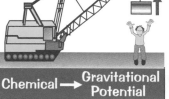
Chemical → Gravitational Potential

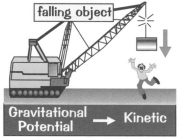
falling object
Gravitational Potential → Kinetic

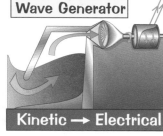
Wave Generator
Kinetic → Electrical

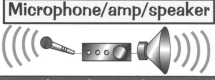
Microphone/amp/speaker
Sound → Electrical → Sound

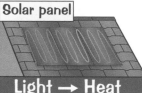
Solar panel

Light → Heat

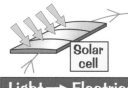
Solar cell
Light → Electrical

wind turbine
Kinetic → Electrical

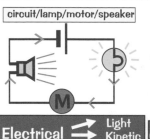
circuit/lamp/motor/speaker
Electrical → Light / Kinetic / Sound

Archer/bow
Chemical → Elastic potential

Bow/arrow
Elastic potential → Kinetic

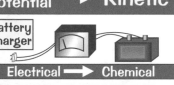
Battery charger
Electrical → Chemical

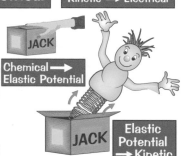
JACK
Chemical → Elastic Potential
Elastic Potential → Kinetic

And DON'T FORGET — ALL types of ENERGY are all measured in JOULES

Learn about Energy — and just keep working at it...

They're pretty keen on the different types of energy and also energy transfers. You'll definitely get an Exam question on it, and if you learn all the stuff on this page, you should have it pretty well covered I'd think. Learn, cover, scribble, check, learn, cover, scribble, etc. etc.

Heat Transfer

There are <u>three</u> distinct methods of heat transfer: <u>conduction</u>, <u>convection</u> *and* <u>radiation</u>.
To answer Exam questions you <u>must</u> use those <u>three key words</u> in just the <u>right places</u>.
And that means you need to know <u>exactly what they are</u>, and all the <u>differences</u> between them.

Heat Energy *Causes* Molecules *to* Move Faster

1) <u>Heat energy</u> causes <u>gas and liquid</u> molecules to move around <u>faster</u>, and causes particles in solids to vibrate <u>more rapidly</u>.

2) When particles move <u>faster</u> it shows up as a <u>rise</u> in temperature.

3) This extra <u>kinetic energy</u> in the particles tends to get <u>dissipated</u> to the <u>surroundings</u>.

4) In other words the <u>heat</u> energy tends to flow <u>away</u> from a hotter object to its <u>cooler</u> surroundings. But then you knew that already. I would hope.

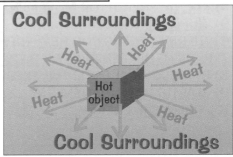

If there's a <u>*DIFFERENCE IN TEMPERATURE*</u> between two places then <u>*HEAT WILL FLOW*</u> between them.

Conduction, Convection *and* Radiation *Compared*

These differences are really important — make sure you <u>learn them</u>:

1) <u>Conduction</u> occurs mainly in <u>solids</u>.

2) <u>Convection</u> occurs mainly in <u>gases and liquids</u>.

3) Gases and liquids are <u>very poor conductors</u> — convection is usually the <u>dominant</u> process. Where convection <u>can't</u> occur, the heat transfer by <u>conduction</u> is <u>very slow</u> indeed:

4) <u>Radiation</u> travels through anything <u>see-through</u> including a <u>vacuum</u>.

5) <u>Heat Radiation</u> is given out by <u>anything</u> which is <u>warm or hot</u>.

6) The <u>amount</u> of heat radiation which is <u>absorbed or emitted</u> depends on the <u>colour</u> and <u>texture</u> of the <u>surface</u>.
But don't forget, <u>convection</u> and <u>conduction</u> are totally <u>unaffected</u> by surface colour or texture. A <u>shiny white</u> surface <u>conducts</u> just as well as a <u>matt black</u> one.

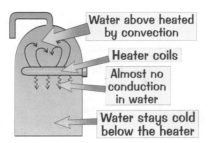

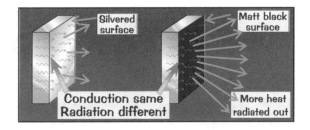

Learn the facts on heat transfer — but don't get a sweat on...

Phew, no more numbers and formulae, now we're back to good old straightforward factual learning again. Much less confusing — but no less of a challenge, it has to be said. You've really got to make a fair old effort to get those three key processes of heat transfer all sorted out in your head so that you know exactly what they are and when they occur. <u>Learn and grin</u>.

Conduction and Convection

Conduction of Heat — Occurs Mainly in Solids

H O T — HEAT FLOW — C O L D

> **CONDUCTION OF HEAT** is the process where *VIBRATING PARTICLES* pass on their *EXTRA VIBRATION ENERGY* to *NEIGHBOURING PARTICLES*.

This process continues throughout the solid and gradually the extra vibrational energy (or heat) is passed all the way through the solid, causing a rise in temperature at the other side.

Non-metals are Good Insulators

1) This normal process of conduction as illustrated above is always very slow.
2) But in most non-metal solids it's the only way that heat can pass through.
3) So non-metals, such as plastic, wood, rubber etc. are very good insulators.
4) Non-metal gases and liquids are even worse conductors, as you will slowly begin to realise if I say it often enough. Metals, on the other hand, are a totally different ball game...

Convection of Heat — Liquids and Gases Only

Gases and liquids are usually free to slosh about — and that allows them to transfer heat by convection, which is a much more effective process than conduction.

Convection simply can't happen in solids because the particles can't move.

> **CONVECTION** occurs when the more energetic particles *MOVE* from the hotter region to the cooler region — *AND TAKE THEIR HEAT ENERGY WITH THEM*

When the more energetic (i.e. hotter) particles get somewhere cooler they then transfer their energy by the usual process of collisions which warm up the surroundings.

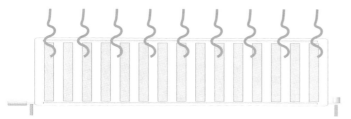

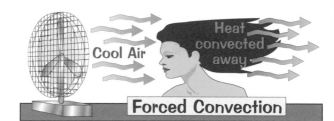

Cool Air — Heat convected away — **Forced Convection**

Convection Currents — easy as a summer evening breeze...

Oi! Watch out! It's another pair of Physics words that look so much alike that half of you think they're the same word. Look: CONVECTION. See, it's different from CONDUCTION. Tricky that one isn't it. Just like reflection and refraction. Not just a different word though, convection is a totally different process too. Make sure you learn exactly why it isn't like conduction.

Heat Radiation

Heat radiation can also be called infrared radiation, and it consists purely of electromagnetic waves of a certain frequency. It's just below visible light in the electromagnetic spectrum.

Heat Radiation *Can Travel Through Vacuum*

Heat radiation is different from the other two methods of heat transfer in quite a few ways:

1) It travels in straight lines at the speed of light.

2) It travels through vacuum. This is the only way that heat can reach us from the Sun.

3) It can be very effectively reflected away again by a silver surface.

4) It only travels through transparent media, like air, glass and water.

5) Its behaviour is strongly dependent on surface colour and texture. This definitely isn't so for conduction and convection.

6) No particles are involved. It's transfer of heat

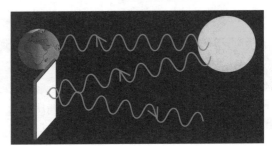

Emission and Absorption of Heat Radiation

1) All objects are continually emitting and absorbing heat radiation.

2) The hotter they are the more heat radiation they emit.

3) Cooler ones around them will absorb this heat radiation. You can feel this heat radiation if you stand near something hot like a fire.

Just a smidge of heat radiation

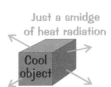

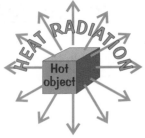

It Depends An Awful Lot on Surface Colour and Texture

1) Dark matt surfaces absorb heat radiation falling on them much more strongly than bright glossy surfaces, such as gloss white or silver. They also emit heat radiation much more too.

2) Silvered surfaces reflect nearly all heat radiation falling on them.

3) In the lab there are several fairly dull experiments to demonstrate the effects of surface on emission and absorption of heat radiation. Here are two of the most gripping:

Leslie's Cube

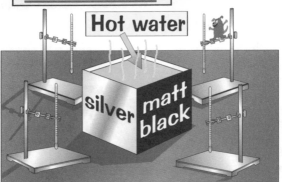

The matt black side emits most heat so it's that thermometer which gets hottest.

The matt black surface absorbs most heat so its wax melts first and the ball bearing drops.

The Melting Wax Trick

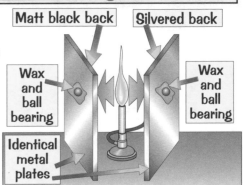

Revise Heat Radiation — absorb as much as you can, anyway...

The main thing to learn here is that heat radiation is strongly affected by the colour and texture of surfaces. Don't forget that the other two types of heat transfer, conduction and convection, are not affected by surface colour and texture at all. Heat radiation is totally different from conduction and convection. Learn all the details on this page, then cover it up and scribble.

Keeping Buildings Warm

Loft Insulation
Initial Cost: £200
Annual Saving: £50
Payback time: 4 years

Hot Water Tank Jacket
Initial Cost: £10
Annual Saving: £15
Payback time: 1 year

Thermostatic Controls
Initial Cost: £100
Annual Saving: £20
Payback time: 5 years

Double Glazing
Initial Cost: £3,000
Annual Saving: £60
Payback time: 50 years

Cavity Wall Insulation
Initial Cost: £500
Annual Saving: £70
Payback time: 7 years

Draught-proofing
Initial Cost: £50
Annual Saving: £50
Payback time: 1 year

Know Which Types of Heat Transfer are Involved:

1) Cavity Wall Insulation — foam squirted into the gap between the bricks reduces convection and radiation across the gap.

2) loft insulation — a thick layer of fibre glass wool laid out across the whole loft floor reduces conduction and radiation into the roof space from the ceiling.

3) Draught proofing — strips of foam and plastic around doors and windows stop draughts of cold air blowing in, i.e. they reduce heat loss due to convection.

4) Double Glazing — two layers of glass with an air gap reduce conduction and radiation.

5) Thermostatic Radiator valves — these simply prevent the house being over-warmed.

6) Hot water tank jacket — lagging such as fibre glass wool reduces conduction and radiation from the hot water tank.

7) Thick Curtains — big bits of cloth you pull across the window to stop people looking in at you, but also to reduce heat loss by conduction and radiation.

They don't seem to have these problems in Spain...

Remember, the most effective insulation measure is the one which keeps the most heat in, (biggest annual saving). If your house had no roof, then a roof would be the most effective measure, would it not! But cost-effectiveness depends very much on the time-scale involved.

Domestic Electricity

Electricity is by far the most _useful_ form of energy. Compared to gas or oil or coal etc. it's _much easier_ to turn it into the _four_ main types of useful energy: _Heat_, _light_, _sound_ and _motion_.

Reading Your Electricity Meter and Working out the Bill

Yip, this is in the syllabus. Don't ask me why, because you never actually need to bother in real life!

$$\boxed{3\ 4\ 6\ 2\ 8\ 7\ 4\ 5} \text{ kW-h}$$

tens   units   tenths of a kW-h

The reading on your meter shows the _total number of units_ (kW-h) used since the meter was fitted. Each bill is worked out from the _increase_ in the meter reading since it was _last read_ for the previous bill.

Kilowatt-hours (kW-h) are "UNITS" of Energy

1) Your electricity meter counts the number of "UNITS" used. A "UNIT" is otherwise known as a _kilowatt-hour_, or _kW-h_. A "_kW-h_" might sound like a unit of power, but it's not — it's an _amount of energy_.

> A _KILOWATT-HOUR_ is the amount of electrical energy used by a _1 KW APPLIANCE_ left on for _1 HOUR_.

2) Make sure you can turn 1 kW-h into 3,600,000 Joules like this:
"E=P×t" =1kW × 1 hour =1000W × 3,600 secs = _3,600,000 J_   (=3.6 MJ)
(The formula is "Energy = Power×time", and the units must be converted to SI first).

The Two Easy Formulae for Calculating The Cost of Electricity

These must surely be the two most _trivial and obvious_ formulae you'll ever see:

No. of _units_ (kW-h) used = _Power_ (in kW) × _Time_ (in hours)	Units = kW × hours
Cost = No. of _UNITS_ × _price_ per UNIT	Cost = Units × Price

N.B.   Always turn the _power_ into _kW_ (not Watts) and the _time_ into _hours_ (not minutes)

Power Ratings of Appliances

A light bulb converts _electrical energy_ into _light_ and has a power rating of 100W which means it transfers _100 joules/second_.

A Kettle converts _electrical energy_ into _heat_ and has a power rating of 3kW, transferring _3000 joules/second_.

The total amount of energy transferred by an appliance therefore depends on _how long_ the appliance is on and its _power rating_ (E=P×t). For example the kettle is on for an hour the energy transferred by the kettle in this time is 3600×3000 = 10800 kJ (3600s = 1 hour).

Kilowa Towers — the Best Lit Hotel in Hawaii...

This page has four sections and you need to learn the stuff in all of them. Start by memorising the headings, then learn the details under each heading. Then _cover the page_ and _scribble down_ what you know. Check back and see what you missed, and then _try again_. And keep trying.

Gravitational Potential Energy

Potential
Energy

Gravitational potential energy might sound a bit tricky, but it's seriously easy:

Gravitational Potential Energy _is_ Energy Due to Height

Gravitational potential energy is the energy stored in an object because it has been raised to a specific height against the force of gravity.

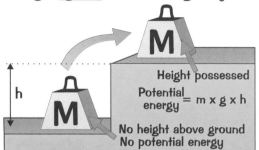

Height possessed

Potential energy = m x g x h

No height above ground
No potential energy

Potential Energy = mass × g × height

Quite often gravitational potential energy is just called "potential energy", but you should use its full name really. The proper name for g is "gravitational field strength".
On Earth this has the value of
$g \approx 10m/s^2$ (N/kg).

Working out Potential Energy

Example: A sheep of mass 47 kg is slowly raised through 6.3 m. Find the gain in potential energy.

Answer: _This is pretty easy._
You just plug the numbers into the formula:
$PE = mgh = 47 \times 10 \times 6.3 = \underline{2961\,J}$

(Joules _again because it's_ energy _again._)

Gravitational Potential Energy can be converted to _Electrical Energy_

1) Most large power stations have huge boilers which have to be kept running all night even though demand is very low. This means there's a surplus of electrical energy at night.

2) It's surprisingly difficult to find a way of storing this spare energy for later use.

3) Pumped storage is one of the best solutions to the problem.

4) In pumped storage "spare" night-time electrical energy is converted to gravitational potential energy by pumping the water up to a higher reservoir against the force of gravity.

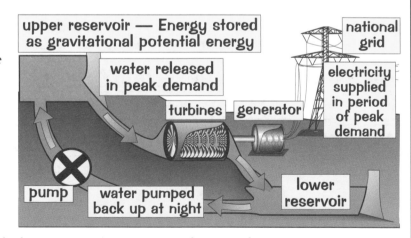

5) The energy is essentially "stored" in the higher reservoir as gravitational potential energy.

6) The water can be released quickly during periods of peak demand such as at tea time each evening.

7) The gravitational potential energy is then converted back to electrical energy at the turbines.

Revise Falling Objects — just don't lose your grip...

It might seem like a tricky subject, but it's not honest. You just need to remember that the higher up you are the more gravitational potential energy you have. It's just two straightforward mini-essays to scribble down, check and learn.

66

Useful Energy Transfers

Efficiency

Most Energy Transfers Involve Some Losses, as Heat

Energy is *ONLY USEFUL* when it's *CONVERTED* from one form to another.

1) Useful devices are only useful because they convert energy from one form to another.
2) In doing so, some of the useful input energy is always lost or wasted as heat.
3) The less energy that is wasted, the more efficient the device is said to be.

4) The energy flow diagram is pretty much the same for all devices. You must learn this basic energy flow diagram:

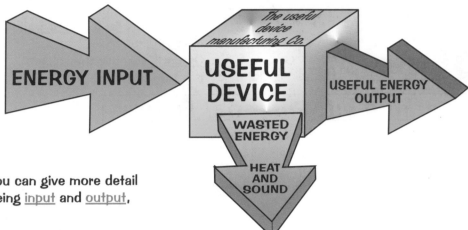

For any specific example you can give more detail about the types of energy being input and output, but remember this:

_NO_ device is 100% efficient and the *WASTED ENERGY* is always *dissipated* as *HEAT* and *SOUND*.

Electric heaters are the exception to this. They're 100% efficient because all the electricity is converted to "useful" heat. What else could it become? Ultimately, all energy ends up as heat energy. If you use an electric drill, it gives out various types of energy but they all quickly end up as heat. The wasted energy and the useful energy both end up just warming the air around us. This energy very quickly spreads out into the surroundings and then it becomes harder and harder to make use of it for further energy transfers. That's an important thing to realise. So realise it — and never forget it.

Don't waste energy — Don't switch anything on

Make sure you know all these easy examples — one of them is bound to come up in your Exams.

Device	Energy Input	Useful Output	Wasted Energy
1) Television	Electrical	Light and Sound	Heat
2) Light Bulb	Electrical	Light	Heat
3) Electric Drill	Electrical	Movement	Heat and Sound
4) Hairdrier	Electrical	Heat	Heat and Sound
5) Car Engine	Chemical	Movement	Heat and Sound
6) Horse	Chemical	Movement and ...	Heat and Sound

Learn about energy dissipation — but keep your cool...

The thing about loss of energy is it's always the same — it always disappears as heat and sound, and even the sound ends up as heat pretty quickly. So when they ask "Why is the input energy more than the output energy?", the answer is always the same... Learn and enjoy.

Power From Non-Renewables

Non-renewable Energy Resources Will Run Out One Day

The non-renewables are the three fossil fuels and nuclear:
1) Coal
2) Oil
3) Natural gas
4) Nuclear fuels (uranium and plutonium)

a) They will all run out one day.
b) They all do damage to the environment.
c) But they provide most of our energy.

Learn the basic features of the typical power station shown here and also the nuclear reactor.

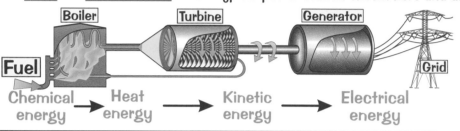

Chemical energy → Heat energy → Kinetic energy → Electrical energy

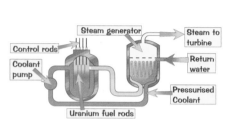

Nuclear Reactors are Just Fancy Boilers

1) A nuclear power station is mostly the same as the one shown above, where heat is produced in a boiler to make steam to drive turbines etc. The difference is in the boiler, as shown here:
2) They take the longest time of all the non-renewables to start up. Natural gas takes the shortest time.

Environmental Problems With The Use Of Non-Renewables

1) All three fossil fuels, (coal, oil and gas) release CO_2. For the same amount of energy produced, coal releases the most CO_2, followed by oil then gas. All this CO_2 adds to the Greenhouse Effect, causing global warming. There's no feasible way to stop it being released either. Ho hum.
2) Burning coal and oil releases sulphur dioxide which causes acid rain. This is reduced by taking the sulphur out before it's burned or cleaning up the emissions.
3) Coal mining makes a mess of the landscape, especially "open-cast mining".
4) Oil spillages cause serious environmental problems. We try to avoid it, but it'll always happen.
5) Nuclear power is clean but the nuclear waste is very dangerous and difficult to dispose of.
6) Nuclear fuel (i.e. uranium) is cheap but the overall cost of nuclear power is high due to the cost of the power plant and final de-commissioning.
7) Nuclear power always carries the risk of major catastrophe like the Chernobyl disaster.

The Non-Renewables Need to be Conserved

1) When the fossil fuels eventually run out we will have to use other forms of energy.
2) To stop the fossil fuels running out so quickly there are two things we can do:

1) Use Less Energy by Being More Efficient With it:

(i) Better insulation of buildings,
(ii) Turning lights and other things off when not needed,
(iii) Making everyone drive spiddly little cars with spacky little engines.

2) Use More Of The Renewable Sources Of Energy

as detailed on the following pages...

Learn about the non-renewables — before it's too late...

Make sure you realise that we generate most of our electricity from the four non-renewables, and that the power stations are all pretty much the same, as exemplified by the above diagram. Also make sure you know all the problems about them and why we should use less of them.

Power from Renewables

Renewable Energy Resources Will Never Run Out

The <u>renewables</u> are:
1) <u>Wind</u>
2) <u>Waves</u>
3) <u>Tides</u>
4) <u>Hydroelectric</u>
5) <u>Solar</u>
6) <u>Geothermal</u>
7) <u>Food</u>
8) <u>Biomass (wood)</u>

a) These will <u>never run out</u>.
b) They <u>do not damage the environment</u> (except visually).
c) The trouble is they <u>don't provide much energy</u> and many of them are <u>unreliable</u> because they depend on the <u>weather</u>.

Wind Power — Lots of Little Wind Turbines

1) This involves putting lots of <u>windmills</u> (wind turbines) up in <u>exposed places</u> like on <u>moors</u> or round <u>coasts</u>.
2) Each wind turbine has its own <u>generator</u> inside it so the electricity is generated <u>directly</u> from the <u>wind</u> turning the <u>blades</u>, which turn the <u>generator</u>. There's <u>no pollution</u>.
3) But they do <u>spoil the view</u>. You need about <u>5000 wind turbines</u> to replace one <u>coal-fired power station</u> and 5000 of them cover <u>a lot</u> of ground — that wouldn't look very nice at all.
4) There's also the problem of <u>no power when the wind stops</u>, and it's <u>impossible</u> to <u>increase supply</u> when there's <u>extra demand</u>.

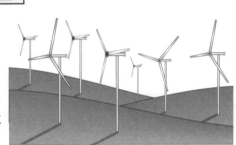

Hydroelectricity — Flooding Valleys

1) <u>Hydroelectric power</u> usually requires the <u>flooding</u> of a valley by building a <u>big dam</u>.
2) <u>Rainwater</u> is caught and allowed out through <u>turbines</u>. There is <u>no pollution</u>.
3) There is quite a <u>big impact</u> on the <u>environment</u> due to the flooding of the valley and possible <u>loss of habitat</u> for some species.
4) A big <u>advantage</u> is <u>immediate response</u> to increased demand and there's no problem with <u>reliability</u> except in times of <u>drought</u> — but remember this is *Scotland* we're talking about!

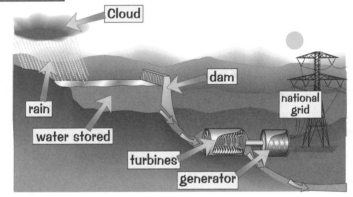

Wood Burning — Environmentally OK

1) It involves the cultivation of <u>fast-growing</u> trees which are then <u>harvested</u>, <u>chopped up</u> and <u>burnt</u> in a power station <u>furnace</u> to produce <u>electricity</u>.
2) The trees are grown as quickly as they are burnt so they will <u>never</u> run out. This does <u>not apply</u> to the burning of <u>rainforests</u> where the trees take <u>much longer</u> to grow.

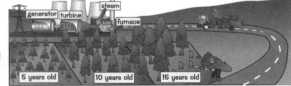

Learn about Wind Power — it can blow your mind...

Lots of important details here on these nice green squeaky clean sources of energy — pity they make such a mess of the landscape. Three nice green squeaky clean <u>mini-essays</u> please.

Power from Renewables

Wave Power — Lots of little Wave Converters

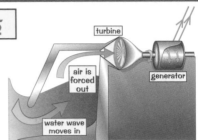

1) You need lots of small <u>wave generators</u> located <u>around the coast</u>.
2) As waves come in to the shore they provide an <u>up and down motion</u> which can be used to drive a <u>generator</u>.
3) They are <u>fairly unreliable</u>, since waves tend to die out when the <u>wind drops</u>.
4) The main environmental problem is <u>spoiling the view</u>.

Tidal Barrages — Using The Sun and Moon's Gravity

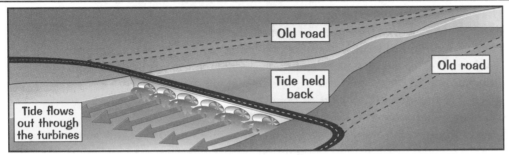

1) <u>Tidal barrages</u> are <u>big dams</u> built across river <u>estuaries</u> with <u>turbines</u> in them.
2) As the tide <u>comes in</u> it fills up the estuary to a height of <u>several metres</u>. This water can then be allowed out through <u>turbines</u> at a controlled speed. It also drives the turbines on the way in.
3) The main problems are <u>preventing free access by boats</u>, <u>spoiling the view</u> and <u>altering the habitat</u> of the wildlife eg: wading birds, sea creatures and beasties who live in the sand.
4) Tides are pretty <u>reliable</u> in the sense that they happen <u>twice a day</u> without fail, and always to the <u>predicted height</u>. The only drawback is that the <u>height</u> of the tide is <u>variable</u> so lower (neap) tides will provide significantly <u>less energy</u> than the bigger "<u>spring</u>" tides. But tidal barrages are excellent for <u>storing energy</u> ready for periods of <u>peak demand</u>.

Solar Energy — Solar Cells

1) <u>SOLAR CELLS</u> generate <u>electric currents directly</u> from sunlight. <u>Initial costs</u> are <u>high</u> but after that the energy is <u>free</u> and <u>running costs almost nil</u>.
2) Despite the cost, solar cells are the <u>best</u> source of energy for <u>calculators</u> and <u>watches</u> which don't use much electricity. Solar power is the only choice for <u>remote places</u> like <u>Antarctica</u> and <u>satellites</u>.
3) Solar cells are the most expensive energy resource <u>per Unit</u> of electricity they produce — except for non–rechargable batteries, of course.
4) There's absolutely <u>no pollution</u> — and in sunny countries solar power is a <u>very reliable</u> source of energy — but only in the <u>daytime</u>.

Geothermal Energy — Heat From Underground

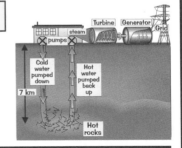

1) This is <u>only possible</u> in places where <u>hot rocks</u> lie quite near the <u>surface</u>. The source of much of the heat is the <u>slow decay</u> of various <u>radioactive elements</u> including <u>uranium</u> deep inside the Earth.
2) <u>Water is pumped</u> down to <u>hot rocks</u> and <u>returns as steam</u> to drive a <u>generator</u>.
3) This is actually <u>free energy</u> with no real environmental problems. The <u>main drawback</u> is the <u>cost of drilling</u> down <u>several km</u> to the hot rocks.

Solar Cells are like Fried Eggs — always best sunny side up...

There's a lot of details here on sources of energy — an awful lot of details. Trouble is, in the Exam they could test you on any of them, so I guess you just gotta learn 'em.

Revision Summary for Module Nine

There are three distinct parts to Module Nine. First there's heat transfer, which is trickier to fully get the grip of than most people realise. Then there's the bits on electricity and gravitational potential energy which is a tad more difficult and finally there's the stuff on useful energy transfers and generating power, which is basically easy but there are lots of drivelly details to learn. Make sure you realise the different approach needed for all three bits and focus your planet-sized brain accordingly.

1) List the ten different types of energy.
2) What's special about chemical and elastic potential energy?
3) Give twelve different examples of energy transfers.
4) What causes heat to flow from one place to another? What do molecules do as they heat up?
5) Explain briefly the difference between conduction, convection and radiation.
6) State which form of heat transfer works through a vacuum.
7) Give a strict definition of conduction of heat and say which materials are good conductors.
8) Name some good insulators. Which bit of a wooden handled spade is the best conductor?
9) Give a description of convection of heat. Is it the same as conduction?
10) List five properties of heat radiation. Which kind of objects emit and absorb heat radiation?
11) Which surfaces absorb heat radiation best? Which surfaces emit it best?
12) Describe two experiments to demonstrate the effect of different surfaces on radiant heat.
13) Describe insulation measures which reduce   a) conduction   b) convection   c) radiation.
14) Name some materials that are good insulators and describe some uses for them in the home.
15) Which types of heat transfer are insulated against in: a) double glazing; b) draught proofing?
16) Which types of heat transfer are insulated against in: a) loft insulation; b) cavity walls?
17) Sketch an electricity meter and explain exactly what the number on it represents.
18) Describe the energy transfers for two typical appliances in the home.
19) What is the formula for determining the energy transfer?
20) What's a kilowatt-hour? What are the two easy formulae for finding the cost of electricity?
21) Give a really easy definition of gravitational potential energy.
22) Who has the largest gravitational potential energy, a man at the top of the Eiffel Tower
     or a man at the bottom?
23) Describe a way of converting gravitational potential energy into electrical energy.
24) Sketch the basic energy flow diagram for a typical "useful device".
25) What forms does the wasted energy always take?
26) Name some household appliances and write down their energy input, useful output energy
     and their wasted energy.
27) List the four non-renewable sources of energy and say why they are non-renewable.
28) Describe some ways that we can conserve the non-renewables.
29) Which kind of resources do we get most of our energy from? Sketch a typical power station.
30) List seven environmental hazards with non-renewables and four ways that we can use less.
31) List the eight kinds of renewable energy resources.
32) Give full details of how we can use wind power, including the advantages and disadvantages.
33) Give full details of how a hydroelectric scheme works.
34) What are the advantages and disadvantages of generating power using hydroelectric schemes?
35) Sketch a wave generator and explain the pros and cons of this as a source of energy.
36) Explain how tidal power can be harnessed. What are the pros and cons of this idea?
37) Explain where geothermal energy comes from. Describe how we can make use of it.
38) Explain the principles of wood-burning for generating electricity.
39) Give brief details, with a diagram, of solar power.

Circuits — The Basics

Circuits

Isn't electricity great. Mind you it's pretty bad news if the words don't mean anything to you...
Hey, I know — learn them now!

1) <u>Current</u> is the <u>flow</u> of electrons round the circuit. Current will <u>only flow</u> through a component if there is a <u>voltage</u> across that component.

2) <u>Voltage</u> is the <u>driving force</u> that pushes the current round. Kind of like 'electrical pressure'.

3) <u>Resistance</u> is anything in the circuit which <u>slows the flow down</u>.

4) <u>There's a balance</u>: the <u>voltage</u> is trying to <u>push</u> the current round the circuit, and the <u>resistance</u> is <u>opposing</u> it — the <u>relative sizes</u> of the voltage and resistance decide <u>how big</u> the current will be:

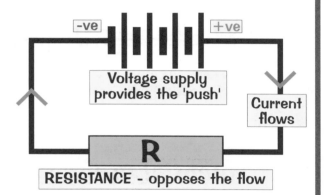

Voltage supply provides the 'push'

Current flows

RESISTANCE - opposes the flow

> If you <u>increase the voltage</u> — then <u>more current</u> will flow.
> If you <u>increase the resistance</u> — then <u>less current</u> will flow
> (or <u>more voltage</u> will be needed to keep the <u>same current</u> flowing).

The Standard Test Circuit

This is without doubt the most totally bog-standard circuit the world has ever known. So know it.

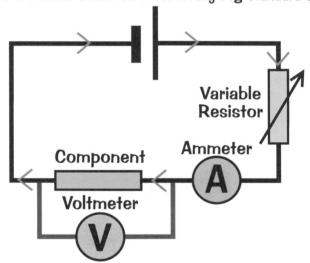

Variable Resistor

Component

Ammeter

Voltmeter

The Ammeter

1) Measures the <u>current</u> (in <u>Amps</u>) flowing through the component.
2) Must be placed <u>in series</u>.
3) Can be put <u>anywhere</u> in series in the <u>main circuit</u>, but <u>never</u> in parallel like the voltmeter.

The Voltmeter

1) Measures the <u>voltage</u> (in <u>Volts</u>) across the component.
2) Must be placed <u>in parallel</u> around the <u>component</u> under test — <u>NOT</u> around the variable resistor or the battery!
3) The <u>proper</u> name for '<u>voltage</u>' is '<u>potential difference</u>' or '<u>p.d.</u>'

Five Important Points

1) This <u>very basic</u> circuit is used for testing <u>components</u>, and for getting <u>V-I graphs</u> for them.
2) The <u>component</u>, the <u>ammeter</u> and the <u>variable resistor</u> are all in <u>series</u>, which means they can be put in <u>any order</u> in the main circuit. The <u>voltmeter</u>, on the other hand, can only be placed <u>in parallel</u> around the <u>component under test</u>, as shown. Anywhere else is a definite <u>no-no</u>.
3) As you <u>vary</u> the <u>variable resistor</u> it alters the <u>current</u> flowing through the circuit.
4) This allows you to take several <u>pairs of readings</u> from the <u>ammeter</u> and <u>voltmeter</u>.
5) You can then <u>plot</u> these values for <u>current</u> and <u>voltage</u> on a <u>V-I graph</u> (see P.77).

Understanding circuits — easy as pie...

This page is all about electric circuits — what they are, how to use them, and how they work. This is the most basic stuff on electricity there is. I assume you realise that you'll never be able to learn anything else about electricity until you know this stuff — don't you? Good-oh.

Series Circuits

You need to be able to tell the difference between series and parallel circuits <u>just by looking at them</u>.
You also need to know the <u>rules</u> about what happens with both types. Read on.

Series Circuits — all or nothing

1) In <u>series circuits</u>, the different components are connected <u>in a line</u>, <u>end to end</u>, between
   the +ve and –ve of the power supply (except for <u>voltmeters</u>, which are always connected
   <u>in parallel</u>, but they don't count as part of the circuit).
2) If you remove or disconnect <u>one</u> component, the circuit is <u>broken</u> and they all <u>stop</u>.
3) This is generally <u>not very handy</u>, and in practice, <u>very few things</u> are connected in series.

1) **Potential Difference is Shared:**

1) In series circuits the <u>total p.d.</u> of the <u>supply</u> is
   <u>shared</u> between the various <u>components</u>

2) The <u>voltages</u> round a series circuit <u>always add
   up</u> to equal the <u>source voltage</u>:

$$V = V_1 + V_2 + V_3$$

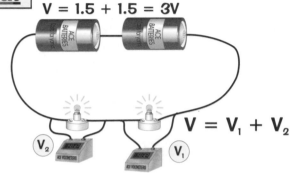

$$V = 1.5 + 1.5 = 3V$$

$$V = V_1 + V_2$$

2) **Current is the Same everywhere:**

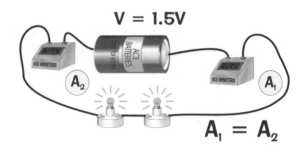

$$V = 1.5V$$

$$A_1 = A_2$$

1) In series circuits the <u>same current</u> flows
   through <u>all parts</u> of the circuit.
   i.e. The reading on ammeter A_1 is the
   same as the reading on ammeter A_2:

$$A_1 = A_2$$

2) The <u>size</u> of the current is determined by the <u>total p.d.</u> of the cells
   and the <u>total resistance</u> of the circuit: i.e. $I = V/R$

3) **Resistance Adds Up:**

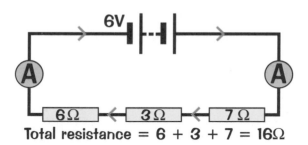

Total resistance = 6 + 3 + 7 = 16Ω

1) In series circuits the <u>total resistance</u> is
   just the <u>sum</u> of all the resistances:

$$R = R_1 + R_2 + R_3$$

2) The <u>bigger</u> the <u>resistance</u> of a component,
   the bigger its <u>share</u> of the <u>total p.d.</u>

Series Circuits

Cell Voltages Add Up:

1) There is a bigger potential difference with more cells in series, provided the cells are all <u>connected</u> the <u>same way</u>.

2) For example when two batteries of voltage 1.5V are <u>connected in series</u> they supply 3V <u>between them</u>.

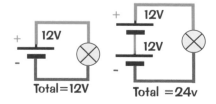

Total=12V   Total =24v

More Lamps in Series means Dimmer Lamps:

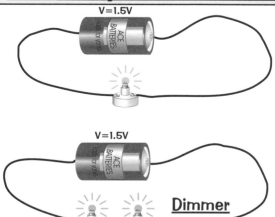

V=1.5V

V=1.5V

<u>Dimmer</u>

1) If a <u>lamp</u> is connected in series with a battery then it lights up with a certain brightness.

2) However with <u>more lamps</u> (of the same resistance) connected in series then all the lamps will light up at a <u>reduced brightness</u>.

3) This is because in a <u>series circuit</u> the voltage is <u>shared out</u> between the components in the circuit.

4) When a <u>second cell</u> is connected in series with the first then the brightness of the lamps will <u>increase</u> because there is a <u>bigger source P.d.</u>

Example on Series Circuits

With the circuit opposite the rules on these two pages apply:

<u>Voltages</u> add to equal the <u>source voltage</u>:
1.5 + 2 + 2.5 = 6V

<u>Total resistance</u> is the sum of the resistances in the circuit: 3 + 4 + 5 = 12 Ohms

<u>Current</u> flowing through all parts of the circuit = V/R = 6/12 = 0.5A

(If an extra cell was added of voltage 3V then the voltage across each resistor would increase).

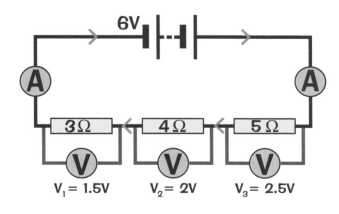

6V

3Ω   4Ω   5 Ω

V_1 = 1.5V V_2= 2V V_3= 2.5V

Christmas Fairy Lights are Wired in Series

<u>Christmas fairy lights</u> are about the <u>only</u> real-life example of things connected in <u>series</u>, and we all know what a <u>pain</u> they are when the <u>whole lot go out</u> just because <u>one</u> of the bulbs is slightly dicky.

The only <u>advantage</u> is that the bulbs can be <u>very small</u> because the total 230V is <u>shared out</u> between them, so each bulb only has a <u>small</u> voltage across it.

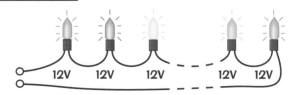

12V 12V 12V   12V 12V

Series Circuits — phew, it's just one thing after another...

They really do want you to know the difference between series and parallel circuits. It's not that tricky but you do have to make a real effort to <u>learn all the details</u>. That's what these pages are for. Learn all those details, then <u>cover the pages</u> and <u>scribble them all down</u>. Then try again...

Parallel Circuits

Parallel circuits are much more sensible than series circuits and so they're much more common in real life.

Parallel Circuits — Independence and Isolation

1) In parallel circuits, each component is separately connected to the +ve and –ve of the supply.
2) If you remove or disconnect one of them, it will hardly affect the others at all.
3) This is obviously how most things must be connected, for example in cars and in household electrics. You have to be able to switch everything on and off separately.

p.d. is the Same across All Components:

1) In parallel circuits all components get the full source p.d., so the voltage is the same across all components:

$$V_1 = V_2 = V_3$$

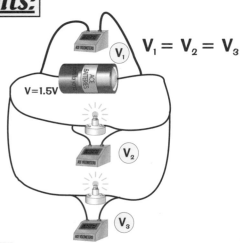

$V_1 = V_2 = V_3$

2) This means that identical bulbs connected in parallel will all be at the same brightness. This is totally different to bulbs connected in series.

Current is Shared between Branches:

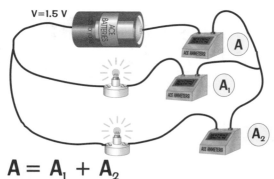

$$A = A_1 + A_2$$

1) In parallel circuits the total current flowing around the circuit is equal to the total of all the currents in the separate branches.

$$A = A_1 + A_2 + A_3$$

2) In a parallel circuit, there are junctions where the current either splits or rejoins. The total current going into a junction always equals the total currents leaving — fairly obviously.

3) If two identical components are connected in parallel then the same current will flow through each component.

Resistance Is Tricky:

1) The current through each component depends on its resistance. The lower the resistance, the bigger the current that'll flow through it.

2) The total resistance of the circuit is tricky to work out, but it's always less than the branch with the smallest resistance.

Parallel Circuits

Parallel Circuits Example

1) The <u>voltage</u> across each resistor in the circuit is the same as the <u>supply voltage</u>.
Each voltmeter will read 6V.

2) The current through each resistor will be <u>different</u> because they have different values of <u>resistance</u>.

3) The current through the battery is the same as the <u>sum</u> of the other currents in the branches.
ie: $A_1 = A_2 + A_3 + A_4$
$A_1 = 1.5 + 3 + 1 = 5.5A$

4) The <u>total resistance</u> in the whole circuit is <u>less</u> than the <u>lowest branch</u>, i.e. lower than 2Ω.

5) The <u>biggest current</u> flows through the <u>middle branch</u> because that branch has the <u>lowest resistance</u>.

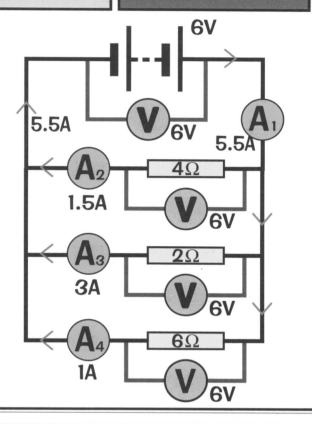

Everything Electrical in a Car is Connected in Parallel

<u>Parallel connection</u> is <u>essential</u> in a car to give these <u>two features</u>:

> 1) Everything can be <u>turned on and off separately</u>.
> 2) Everything always gets the <u>full voltage</u> from the battery.

The only <u>slight effect</u> is that when you turn <u>lots of things on</u> the lights may go <u>dim</u> because the battery can't provide <u>full voltage</u> under <u>heavy load</u>. This is normally a <u>very slight</u> effect. You can spot the same thing at home when you turn a kettle on, if you watch very carefully.

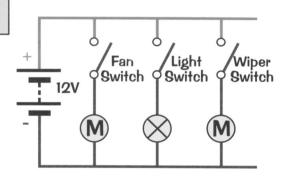

Voltmeters and Ammeters are Exceptions to the rule:

1) Ammeters and Voltmeters are <u>exceptions</u> to the series and parallel rules.
2) Ammeters are <u>always</u> connected in <u>series</u> even in a parallel circuit.
3) Voltmeters are <u>always</u> connected in <u>parallel with a component</u> even in a series circuit.

Electric Circuits — unparalleled dreariness...

Make sure you can scribble down a parallel circuit and know what the advantages are. Learn the five numbered points and the details for connecting ammeters and voltmeters, and also what two features make parallel connection essential in a car. Then <u>cover the page</u> and <u>scribble it</u>...

Circuit Symbols and Devices

Circuit Symbols You Should Know:

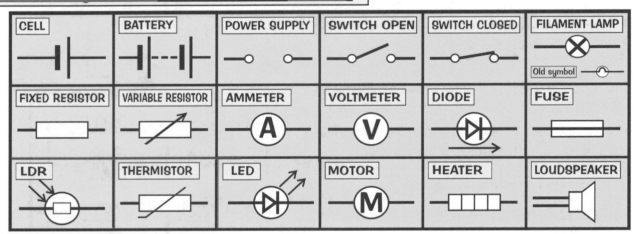

CELL	BATTERY	POWER SUPPLY	SWITCH OPEN	SWITCH CLOSED	FILAMENT LAMP
FIXED RESISTOR	VARIABLE RESISTOR	AMMETER	VOLTMETER	DIODE	FUSE
LDR	THERMISTOR	LED	MOTOR	HEATER	LOUDSPEAKER

1) Variable Resistor

1) A resistor whose resistance can be changed by twiddling a knob or something.
2) The old-fashioned ones are huge coils of wire with a slider on them.
3) They're great for altering the current flowing through a circuit.
   Turn the resistance up, the current drops. Turn the resistance down, the current goes up.

2) Semiconductor Diode or just 'Diode'

A special device made from semiconductor material such as silicon.
It lets current flow freely through it in one direction, but not in the
other (i.e. there's a very high resistance in the reverse direction).
This turns out to be really useful in various electronic circuits.

3) Light Dependent Resistor or 'LDR' to you

1) In bright light, the resistance falls.
2) In darkness, the resistance is highest.
3) This makes it a useful device for various
   electronic circuits
   eg: automatic night lights, burglar detectors.

4) Thermistor (Temperature-dependent Resistor)

1) In hot conditions, the resistance drops.
2) In cool conditions, the resistance goes up.
3) Thermistors make useful temperature detectors,
   eg: car engine temperature sensors and
   electronic thermostats.

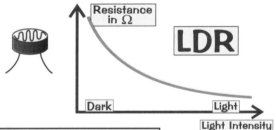

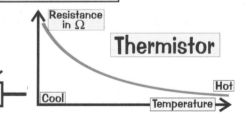

'Diode' — wasn't that a film starring Bruce Willis...

Another page of basic but important details about electrical circuits. You need to know all those
circuit symbols as well as the extra details for the four special devices. When you think you
know it all try covering the page and scribbling it all down. See how you did, and then try again.

Resistance and V=I×R

Four Hideously Important Voltage-Current Graphs

V-I graphs show how the current varies as you change the voltage. Learn these four real well:

Resistor

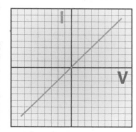

Different Wires

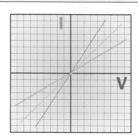

Filament Lamp

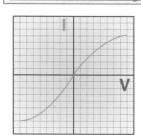

Diode

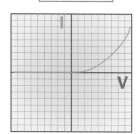

Explaining the graphs above:

Resistor

The current through a resistor (at constant temperature) is proportional to voltage.

Different Wires

Different wires have different resistances, hence the different slopes.

Filament Lamp

As the temperature of the filament increases, the resistance increases, hence the curve.

Diode

Current will only flow through a diode in one direction, as shown.

Calculating Resistance: R =V/I, (or R ='1/gradient')

For the straight-line graphs the resistance of the component is steady and is equal to the inverse of the gradient of the line, or '1/gradient'. In other words, the steeper the graph the lower the resistance.

If the graph curves, it means the resistance is changing. In that case R can be found for any point by taking the pair of values (V,I) from the graph and sticking them in the formula R =V/I. Easy.

$$Resistance = \frac{Potential\ Difference}{Current}$$

Calculating Resistance — An Example

EXAMPLE. Voltmeter V reads 6V and resistor R is 4Ω, what is the current through Ammeter A ?

ANSWER. Taking the formula V = I×R, we need to find I so the version we need is I = V/R.
The answer is then: 6/4 which is 1½ A.

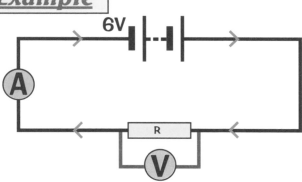

In the end, you'll have to learn this — resistance is futile...

There are quite a lot of important details on this page and you need to learn all of them.
The only way to make sure you really know it is to cover up the page and see how much of it you can scribble down from memory. Sure, it's not that easy — but it's the only way. Enjoy.

Electrolysis

In the two examples below the charges are <u>free</u> to move in the substance in which they are formed.

In <u>Metals</u> the <u>Current</u> is <u>Carried</u> by <u>Electrons</u>

1) Electric current will only flow if there are <u>charges</u> which can <u>move freely</u>.
2) Metals contain a <u>'sea' of free electrons</u> (which are negatively charged) and which <u>flow</u> throughout the metal.
3) This is what allows <u>electric current</u> to flow so well in <u>all</u> metals.

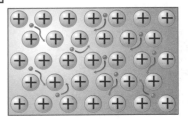

In <u>Electrolytes</u>, <u>Current</u> is <u>Carried</u> by <u>Both</u> +ve and –ve <u>Charges</u>

1) Copper chloride will <u>not conduct</u> electricity in its normal state as a <u>solid</u> because there are <u>no free charges</u> moving around.

2) In order for copper chloride to conduct electricity then charges need to be able to <u>flow freely</u> in the substance, this is achieved by either dissolving the substance in water or heating it until it is molten.

3) The substance then becomes an <u>electrolyte</u>:

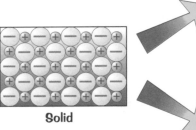

Solid

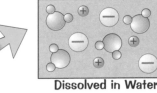

Dissolved in Water

Melted

<u>Electrolytes</u> can <u>Conduct</u> Electricity

1) <u>Electrolytes</u> are liquids which contain charges which can <u>move freely</u>.

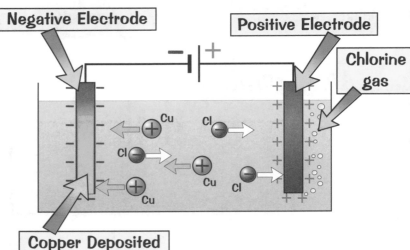

Negative Electrode

Positive Electrode

Chlorine gas

Copper Deposited

2) When a voltage is applied across the liquid the <u>positive</u> charges move towards the <u>–ve</u> electrode, and the <u>negative</u> charges move towards the <u>+ve</u> electrode. This is an <u>electric current</u>.

3) This process is called <u>electrolysis</u>. The substance is now conducting electricity.

4) Substances form at the electrodes during this process, for example in copper chloride solution, <u>Copper</u> forms at the <u>negative electrode</u>.

Electrolysis — time to recharge those batteries...

Just three simple mini-essays to rewrite with all those lovely important points to remember. Learn the details then go for a quick walk, come back and write it all down. Check back to see what you missed, then try again.

Static Electricity

Static electricity is all about charges which are <u>not</u> free to move. This causes them to build up in one place and it often ends with a <u>spark</u> or a <u>shock</u> when they do finally move.

1) *Build up of Static is Caused by Friction*

1) When two <u>insulating</u> materials are <u>rubbed</u> together, electrons will be <u>scraped off one</u> and <u>dumped</u> on the other.

2) This'll leave a <u>positive</u> static charge on one and a <u>negative</u> static charge on the other.

3) <u>Which way</u> the electrons are transferred <u>depends</u> on the <u>two materials</u> involved.

4) Electrically charged objects <u>attract</u> small objects placed near them.
(Try this: rub a balloon on a woolly pully – then put it near tiddly bits of paper and watch them jump.)

5) The classic examples are <u>polythene</u> and <u>acetate</u> rods being rubbed with a <u>cloth duster</u>, as shown in the diagrams:

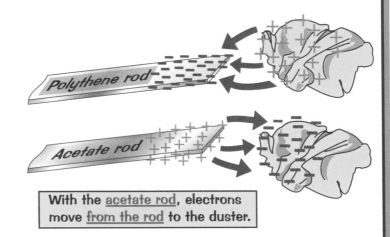

With the <u>polythene rod</u>, electrons move <u>from the duster</u> to the rod.

With the <u>acetate rod</u>, electrons move <u>from the rod</u> to the duster.

2) *Only Electrons Move — Never the Positive Charges*

<u>Watch out for this in Exams</u>. Both +ve and –ve electrostatic charges are only ever produced by the movement of <u>electrons</u>. The positive charges <u>definitely do not move</u>! A positive static charge is always caused by electrons <u>moving</u> away elsewhere, as shown above. Don't forget!

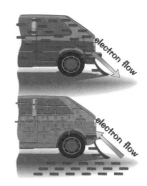

3) *Discharging — Use an Earthing Strap*

A charged conductor can be <u>discharged safely</u> by connecting it to earth with a <u>metal strap</u>. The electrons flow <u>down</u> the strap to the ground if the charge is <u>negative</u> and flow <u>up</u> the strap from the ground if the charge is <u>positive</u>.

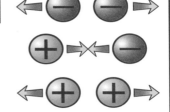

4) *Like Charges Repel, Opposite Charges Attract*

This is <u>easy</u> and, I'd have thought, <u>kind of obvious</u>.
Two things with <u>opposite</u> electric charges are <u>attracted</u> to each other.
Two things with the <u>same</u> electric charge will <u>repel</u> each other.
These forces get <u>weaker</u> the <u>further apart</u> the two things are.

Phew — it's enough to make your hair stand on end...

The way to tackle this page is to first <u>learn the four headings</u> till you can <u>scribble them all down</u>. Then learn the details for each one, and keep practising by <u>covering the page</u> and scribbling down each heading with as many details as you can remember for each one. Just <u>keep trying</u>...

Static Electricity — Examples

They like asking you to give <u>quite detailed examples</u> in Exams. Make sure you <u>learn all these details</u>.

Static Electricity Being Helpful:

1) Inkjet Printer:

1) Tiny droplets of ink are forced out of a <u>fine nozzle</u>, making them <u>electrically charged</u>.
2) The droplets are <u>deflected</u> as they pass between two metal plates. A <u>voltage</u> is applied to the plates — one is <u>negative</u> and the other is <u>positive</u>.
3) The droplets are <u>attracted</u> to the plate of the <u>same</u> charge and <u>repelled</u> from the plate with the <u>opposite</u> charge.
4) The <u>size</u> and <u>direction</u> of the voltage across each plate changes so each droplet is deflected to hit a <u>different place</u> on the paper.
5) Loads of tiny dots make up your print-out. Clever.

+ve / jet of ink / -ve / printout

2) Photocopier:

1) The <u>metal plate</u> is electrically charged. An image of what you're copying is projected onto it.
2) Whiter bits of the thing you're copying make <u>light</u> fall on the plate and the charge <u>leaks away</u>.
3) The charged bits attract <u>black powder</u>, which is transferred onto paper.
4) The paper is <u>heated</u> so the powder sticks.
5) Voilà, a photocopy of your piece of paper (or whatever else you've shoved in there).

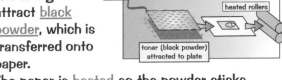
light / -ve / heated rollers / toner (black powder) attracted to plate

3) Spray Painting and Dust Removal in Chimneys...
But photocopiers and inkjet printers are what they <u>really</u> want you to learn.

Static Electricity Being a Little Joker:

1) Car Shocks

<u>Air rushing past</u> your car can give it a <u>+ve charge</u>. When you get out and touch the <u>door</u> it gives you a real buzz — in the Exam make sure you say "<u>electrons</u> flow from earth, through you, to <u>neutralise</u> the +ve charge on the car. Some cars have <u>conducting rubber strips</u> which hang down behind the car. This gives a <u>safe discharge</u> to earth, but spoils all the fun.

2) Clothing Crackles

When <u>synthetic clothes</u> are <u>dragged</u> over each other (like in a <u>tumble drier</u>) or over your <u>head</u>, electrons get scraped off, leaving <u>static charges</u> on both parts, and that leads to the inevitable — <u>attraction</u> (they stick together) and little <u>sparks</u> / <u>shocks</u> as the charges <u>rearrange themselves</u>.

Static Electricity Playing at Terrorist:

1) Lightning
Rain droplets fall to Earth with <u>positive charge</u>. This creates a <u>huge voltage</u> and a <u>big spark</u>.

2) Grain Shoots, Paper Rollers and The Fuel Filling Nightmare:

1) As <u>fuel</u> flows out of a <u>filler pipe</u>, or <u>paper</u> drags over <u>rollers</u>, or <u>grain</u> shoots out of <u>pipes</u>, then <u>static can build up</u>.
2) This can easily lead to a <u>spark</u> and in <u>dusty</u> or <u>fumey</u> places — BOOM!
3) <u>The solution</u>: make the nozzles or rollers out of <u>metal</u> so that the charge is <u>conducted away</u>, instead of building up.
4) It's also good to have <u>earthing straps</u> between the <u>fuel tank</u> and the <u>fuel pipe</u>.

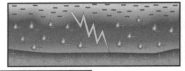
grain chute / paper rollers
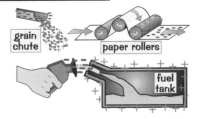
fuel tank

Static Electricity — learn the shocking truth...

You <u>really</u> need to learn those two big examples at the top. <u>All</u> the syllabuses mention photocopiers and inkjet printers so there's <u>bound</u> to be a question. Good grief, it's almost relevant to real-life too. Learn the numbered points and keep scribbling them down to check.

Mains Electricity

Now then, did you know... electricity is dangerous. It can kill you. Well just watch out for it, that's all.

Hazards in The Home — Eliminate Them before They Eliminate You

A likely Exam question will show you a picture of domestic bliss but with various electrical hazards in the picture such as kids shoving their fingers into sockets and stuff like that, and they'll ask you to list all the hazards. This should be mostly common sense, but it won't half help if you've already learnt this list:

1) Long cables or frayed cables.
2) Cables in contact with something hot or wet.
3) Pet rabbits or children (always hazardous).
4) Water near sockets, or shoving things into sockets.
5) Damaged plugs, or too many plugs into one socket.
6) Lighting sockets without bulbs in.
7) Appliances without their covers on.

Plugs and Cables — Learn the Safety Features

Get the Wiring Right:

1) The right coloured wire to each pin, and firmly screwed in.
2) No bare wires showing inside the plug.
3) Cable grip tightly fastened over the cable outer layer.

Plug Features:

1) The metal parts are made of copper or brass because these are very good conductors.
2) The case, cable grip and cable insulation are all made of plastic because this is a really good insulator and is flexible too.
3) This all keeps the electricity flowing where it should.

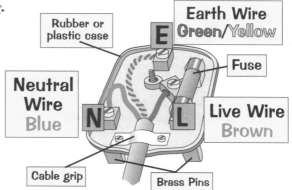

Plug Wiring Errors

They're pretty keen on these diagrams in the Exam so make sure you know them.
The diagram above shows how to wire a plug properly.
Shown below are examples of how not to wire a plug.
A badly wired plug is real dangerous so learn these diagrams.

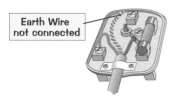
Earth Wire not connected

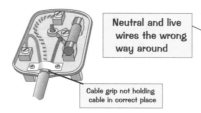
Cable grip not holding cable in correct place

Neutral and live wires the wrong way around

Bare wires showing

Some people are so careless with electricity — it's shocking...

Make sure you can list all those hazards in the home. Make sure you know all the details for wiring a plug. Trickiest of all, make sure you can spot when a plug is not wired properly and how to fix it. Learnt it all? Good-O. So cover the page and scribble it all down again.

Mains, Fuses and Earthing

Mains Supply is AC, Battery supply is DC

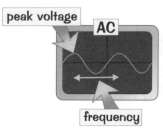

1) The U.K. mains supply is 230 – 240 Volts.

2) It is an <u>AC supply</u> (alternating current), which means the current is <u>constantly</u> changing direction. The <u>CRO trace</u> is <u>always a wave</u>.

3) The frequency of the AC mains supply is <u>50 cycles per second or 50Hz</u>.

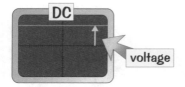

4) By contrast, cells and batteries supply <u>direct current</u> (DC). This just means that the current keeps flowing in the <u>same direction</u>. The <u>CRO trace</u> is a <u>horizontal line</u>.

You need to <u>learn</u> these CRO traces — I've not put them in cos they're pretty.

Fuses prevent Electric Shocks

1) To prevent <u>surges of current</u> in electrical circuits and danger of electric shocks, a fuse is normally placed in the circuit.

2) If the current in the circuit <u>gets too big</u> (bigger than the fuse rating), the fuse wire <u>heats up</u> and the <u>fuse blows</u> breaking the circuit thus preventing any electric shocks.

3) <u>Fuses</u> should be <u>rated</u> as near as possible but just <u>higher</u> than the normal <u>operating current</u>.

4) The fuse should always be the <u>same value</u> as the manufacturer recommends.

Earthing prevents Fires and Shocks

Electricity normally flows <u>in</u> and <u>out</u> through the <u>LIVE</u> and <u>NEUTRAL</u> wires only. The <u>EARTH WIRE</u> and <u>fuse</u> (or circuit breaker, see P.87) are just for <u>safety</u> and work together like this:

1) The earth pin is <u>connected</u> to the case via the <u>earth wire</u> (the yellow and green wire).

2) If a <u>fault</u> develops in which the <u>live</u> somehow touches the <u>metal case</u>, then because the case is <u>earthed</u>, a <u>big current</u> flows in through the <u>live</u>, through the <u>case</u> and out down the <u>earth wire</u>.

3) This <u>surge</u> in current <u>blows the fuse</u> (or trips the circuit breaker), which <u>cuts off</u> the <u>live supply</u>. This prevents electric shocks from the case.

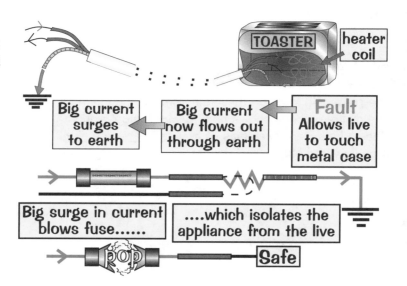

All appliances with <u>metal cases</u> must be 'earthed' to avoid the danger of <u>electric shock</u>. 'Earthing' just means the metal case must be <u>attached</u> to the <u>earth wire</u> in the cable.

Mains Supply and Fuses — what on Earth is it all about...

Well there you go, three important sections rolled onto one page. Learn the details under each heading, cover up the page and scribble it down. Make sure you can sketch those CRO screen traces too. If you don't get it the first time check back and try again.

Energy and Fuses

Energy in Circuits

You can look at <u>electrical circuits</u> in <u>two ways</u>.
The first is in terms of a voltage <u>pushing the current</u> round and the resistances opposing the flow, as on P. 74.
The <u>other way</u> of looking at circuits is in terms of <u>energy transfer</u>.
Learn them <u>both</u> and be ready to tackle questions about <u>either</u>.

Energy *is* Transferred *from Cells and Other Sources*

Anything which <u>supplies electricity</u> is also supplying <u>energy</u>. So cells, batteries, generators etc. all <u>transfer energy</u> to components in the circuit. <u>Learn these as examples</u>:

Motion: motors
Light: light bulbs
Heat: Hairdriers/kettles
Sound: speakers

 Kinetic Energy
 Light Energy
 Cell provides the energy
 Heat Energy
 Sound Energy

All Resistors produce Heat when a Current flows through them

1) This is important.
   Whenever a <u>current</u> flows through anything with <u>electrical resistance</u> (which is pretty well <u>everything</u>) then <u>electrical energy</u> is converted into <u>heat energy</u>.

2) The <u>more current</u> that flows, the <u>more heat</u> is produced.

Calculating Electrical Power and Fuse ratings

1) The standard formula for working out electrical power is:

 P=V×I

2) Most electrical goods indicate their <u>power rating</u> and <u>voltage rating</u>. To work out the <u>fuse</u> needed, you need to work out the <u>current</u> that the item will normally use. That means using 'P=VI', or rather, 'I=P/V'.

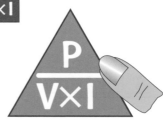

<u>EXAMPLE</u>: *A hairdrier is rated at 240V, 1.1kW. Find the fuse needed.*
<u>ANSWER</u>: I = P/V =1100/240 = 4.6A. Normally, the fuse should be rated just a little higher than the normal current, so a 5 amp fuse is ideal for this one.

Mains Supply and Fuses — what on Earth is it all about...

Well there you go, six important sections rolled onto one page. Make sure you remember the important formula in the middle there. Learn the details under each heading, cover up the page and scribble it down. If you don't get it the first time check back and try again.

Magnetic Fields

There's a proper definition of a <u>magnetic field</u> which you really ought to learn:

> A <u>magnetic field</u> is a region where <u>magnetic materials</u> (like iron and steel) and also <u>wires carrying currents</u> experience <u>a force</u> acting on them.

Learn all These *Magnetic Field Diagrams, Arrow-perfect*

They're real likely to give you one of these diagrams to do in your Exam.
So make sure you know them, especially which way the <u>arrows point</u> — <u>always from N to S!</u>

Bar Magnet

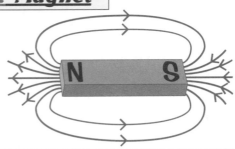

Solenoid

Same field as a bar magnet <u>outside</u>.

<u>Strong and uniform</u> field on the <u>inside</u>.

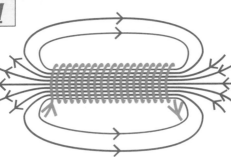

Two Bar Magnets Attracting

<u>Opposite poles attract</u>, as I'm sure you know.

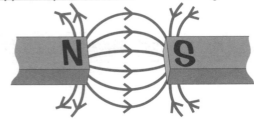

Two Bar Magnets Repelling

<u>Like poles repel</u>, as you must surely know.

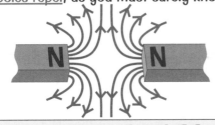

The Earth's Magnetic Field

Note that the <u>magnetic poles</u> are <u>opposite</u> to the <u>Geographic Poles</u>, i.e. the <u>south pole</u> is at the <u>North Pole</u> — if you see what I mean!

The Magnetic Field Round a Current-carrying Wire

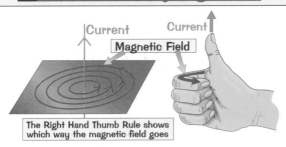

The Right Hand Thumb Rule shows which way the magnetic field goes

A Plotting Compass *is a Freely Suspended Magnet*

1) This means it always <u>aligns</u> itself with the <u>magnetic field</u> that it's in.
2) This is great for plotting <u>magnetic field lines</u> like around the <u>bar magnets</u> shown above.
3) Away from any magnets, it will <u>align</u> with the magnetic field of the <u>Earth</u> and point <u>North</u>.
4) <u>Any magnet</u> suspended so it can turn <u>freely</u> will also come to rest pointing <u>North-South</u>.
5) The end of the magnet which points North is called a '<u>North-seeking pole</u>' or '<u>magnetic North</u>'.
   The end pointing South will therefore be a '<u>magnetic South pole</u>'. This is how they got their names.

Magnetic fields — there's no getting away from them...

Mmm, this is a nice easy page for you isn't it. Learn the definition of what a magnetic field is and the six field diagrams. Also learn those five details about plotting compasses and which way the poles are compared to the Earth. Then <u>cover the page</u> and <u>scribble it all down</u>.

Electromagnets

An Electromagnet is just a Coil of Wire with an Iron Core

1) Electromagnets are really simple.
2) They're simply a solenoid (which is just a coil of wire) with a piece of 'soft' iron inside.
3) When current flows through the wires of the solenoid it creates a magnetic field around it.
4) The soft iron core has the effect of increasing the magnetic field strength.

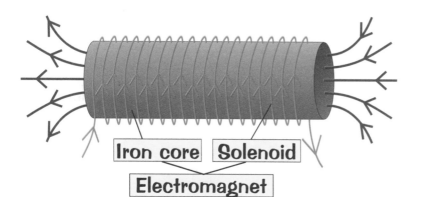

Iron core | Solenoid

Electromagnet

1) The magnetic field around an electromagnet is just like the one round a bar magnet, only it can be made much stronger.

2) This means that the ends of a solenoid act like the North Pole and South Pole of a bar magnet.

3) Pretty obviously, if the direction of the current is reversed, the N and S poles will swap ends.

4) If you imagine looking directly into one end of a solenoid, the direction of current flow tells you whether it's the N or S pole you're looking at, as shown by the two diagrams opposite. You need to remember those diagrams. They may show you a solenoid in the Exam and ask you which pole it is.

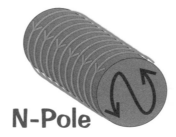
N-Pole

S-Pole

The STRENGTH of an ELECTROMAGNET increases if you:

1) Increase the size of the current.
2) Increase the number of turns the coil has.
3) Replace the core with an iron core.

Iron is Magnetically 'Soft' — Ideal for Electromagnets

In magnetic terms, 'soft' means it changes easily between being magnetised and demagnetised. Iron is 'soft' which makes it perfect for electromagnets which need to be turned on and off.

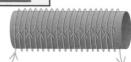

Steel is Magnetically 'Hard' — Ideal for Permanent Magnets

Magnetically 'hard' means that the material retains its magnetism. This would be hopeless in an electromagnet, but is exactly what's required for permanent magnets.

N   S

Electromagnets really irritate me — I just get solenoid with them...

This is all very basic information, and really quite memorable I'd have thought. Learn the headings and diagrams first, then cover the page and scribble them down. Then gradually fill in the other details. Keep looking back and checking. Try to learn all the points. Lovely innit.

The Motor Effect

Anything carrying a <u>current</u> in a <u>magnetic field</u> will experience a <u>force</u>. There are <u>three important cases</u>:

A Current in a Magnetic Field Experiences a Force

The two tests below demonstrate the <u>force</u> on a <u>current-carrying wire</u> placed in a <u>magnetic field</u>.
The <u>force</u> gets <u>bigger</u> if either the <u>current</u> or the <u>magnetic field</u> is made bigger.

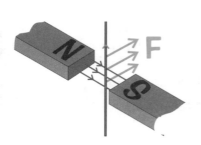

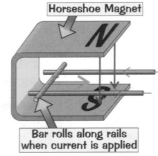

Horseshoe Magnet

Bar rolls along rails
when current is applied

1) Note that in <u>both cases</u> the <u>force</u> on the wire is at <u>90°</u> to both the <u>wire</u> and to the <u>magnetic field</u>.
2) You can always <u>predict</u> which way the <u>force</u> will act using <u>Fleming's LHR</u> as shown below.
3) To experience the <u>full force</u>, the <u>wire</u> has to be at <u>90°</u> to the <u>magnetic field</u>.
4) The <u>direction</u> of the force is <u>reversed</u> if either:
   a) the direction of the <u>current</u> is reversed.
   b) the direction of the <u>magnetic field</u> is reversed.

The Simple Electric Motor

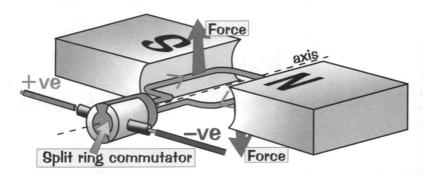

Force

axis

+ve

−ve

Split ring commutator

Force

4 Factors which Speed it up

1) More <u>current</u>
2) More <u>turns</u> on the coil
3) <u>Stronger Magnetic field</u>
4) A <u>soft Iron Core</u> in the coil

1) The diagram shows the <u>forces</u> acting on the two <u>side arms</u> of the <u>coil</u>.
2) These forces are just the <u>usual forces</u> which act on <u>any current</u> in a <u>magnetic field</u>.
3) Because the coil is on a <u>spindle</u> and the forces act <u>one up</u> and <u>one down</u>, it <u>rotates</u>.
4) The direction of the motor can be <u>reversed</u> either by swapping the <u>polarity</u> of the <u>DC supply</u> or swapping the <u>magnetic poles</u> over.

Fleming's Left Hand Rule *tells you* Which way the Force Acts

1) They could test if you can do this, so <u>practise it</u>.
2) Using your <u>left hand</u>, point your <u>First finger</u> in the direction of the <u>Field</u> and your <u>seCond finger</u> in the direction of the <u>Current</u>.
3) Your <u>thumb</u> will then point in the direction of the <u>force</u> *(motion)*.

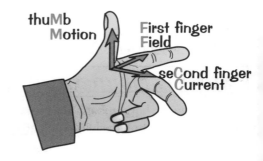

thuMb
Motion

First finger
Field

seCond finger
Current

Fleming!— how many broken wrists has he caused already...

Same old routine here. <u>Learn all the details</u>, diagrams and all, then <u>cover the page</u> and <u>scribble it all down</u> again <u>from memory</u>. I presume you do realise that you should be scribbling it down as scruffy as you like — because all you're trying to do is make sure that you really do <u>know it</u>.

Electromagnetic Devices

Electromagnets always have a soft iron core, which increases the strength of the magnet. The core has to be soft (magnetically soft, that is), so that when the current is turned off, the magnetism disappears with it. The four applications below depend on that happening.

Loudspeakers

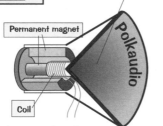

1) AC electrical signals from the amplifier are fed to the speaker coil (shown red).

2) These make the coil move back and forth over the North pole of the magnet.

3) These movements make the cardboard cone vibrate and this creates sounds.

Circuit Breaker — or resettable fuse.

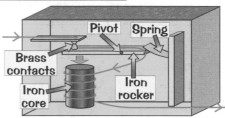

1) This is placed on the incoming live wire.
2) If the current gets too high, the magnetic field in the coil pulls the iron rocker which 'trips' the switch and breaks the circuit.
3) It can be reset manually, but will always flick itself off if the current is too high.

Relay

Eg: A big relay is used for safety in cars for switching the starter motor, because it draws a very big current.

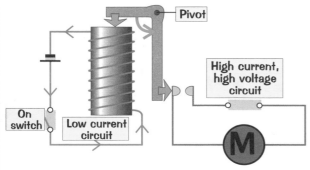

1) A relay is a device which uses a low current circuit to switch a high current circuit on/off.
2) When the switch in the low current circuit is closed it turns the electromagnet on which attracts the iron rocker.
3) The rocker pivots and closes the contacts in the high current circuit.
4) When the low current switch is opened, the electromagnet stops pulling, the rocker returns, and the high current circuit is broken again.

Electric Bell — These are used in schools to stress everyone out.

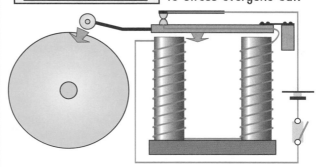

1) When the switch is closed, the electromagnets are turned on.
2) They pull the iron arm down which clangs the bell, but at the same time breaks the contact, which immediately turns off the electromagnets.
3) The arm then springs back, which closes the contact, and off we go again...
4) The whole sequence happens very quickly, maybe 10 times a second, so the bell sounds like a continuous "brrriiiinnngg" sound. Nice.

Only Iron, Steel and Nickel are Magnetic

Don't forget that only iron, steel and nickel experience a force from a magnet. So a magnet won't stick to aluminium ladders or copper kettles or brass trumpets or gold rings or silver spoons.

Learn about Magnets — it'll save you coming unstuck...

They nearly always have one of these in the Exam. Usually it's a circuit diagram of one of them and likely as not they'll ask you to explain exactly how it works. Make sure you learn all those tricky details for each of them. Cover, scribble, etc...

Electromagnetic Induction

Sounds terrifying. Well sure it's quite mysterious, but it isn't that complicated:

Electromagnetic Induction: The creation of a <u>voltage</u> (and maybe current) in a wire which is experiencing a <u>change in magnetic field</u>.

For some reason they use the word '<u>induction</u>' rather than '<u>creation</u>', but it amounts to the <u>same thing</u>.

EM Induction — a) Flux cutting   b) Field Through a Coil

<u>Electromagnetic induction</u> is the <u>induction</u> of a <u>voltage</u> and/or <u>current</u> in a conductor.
There are <u>two different situations</u> where you get <u>EM induction</u>. You need to know about <u>both</u> of them:
   a) The <u>conductor</u> moves across a <u>magnetic field</u> and '<u>cuts</u>' through the lines of <u>magnetic flux</u>.
   b) The <u>magnetic field</u> through a <u>closed coil</u> changes, i.e. gets <u>bigger</u> or <u>smaller</u> or <u>reverses</u>.

Induced voltage

If the direction of <u>movement</u> is <u>reversed</u>, then the induced <u>voltage/current</u> will be <u>reversed</u> too.

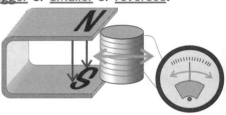

Generators and Dynamos

1) Generators <u>rotate a coil</u> in a <u>magnetic field</u>.
2) Their <u>construction</u> is pretty much like a <u>motor</u>.
3) The difference is the <u>slip rings</u> which means they produce <u>AC voltage</u>, as shown by the <u>CRO displays</u>.
  Note: <u>faster revs</u> produce not only <u>more peaks</u> but <u>higher overall voltage</u> too.

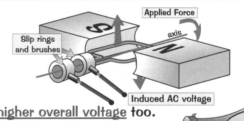

Applied Force / axis / Slip rings and brushes / Induced AC voltage

<u>Dynamos</u> are slightly different from <u>generators</u> because they rotate the <u>magnet</u>. This still causes the <u>field through the coil</u> to <u>swap</u> every half turn, so the output is <u>just the same</u>, as shown in the CRO displays above.

Transformers Change Voltage — but only AC

<u>Transformers</u> use <u>Electromagnetic Induction</u>. So they will <u>only</u> work on <u>AC</u>.

1) Transformers are used to <u>change voltage</u>. They can either <u>increase it</u> or <u>decrease it</u>. <u>Step-up</u> transformers step the voltage <u>up</u>. <u>Step-down</u> transformers step it <u>down</u>.
2) They work using <u>electromagnetic induction</u>.
3) The <u>laminated iron core</u> is purely for transferring the <u>magnetic field</u> from the primary coil to the secondary coil.
4) No <u>electricity</u> flows round the <u>iron core</u>, only <u>magnetic field</u>.
5) The iron core is <u>laminated</u> with <u>layers of insulation</u> to reduce the <u>eddy currents</u> which <u>heat it up</u>, and therefore <u>waste energy</u>.

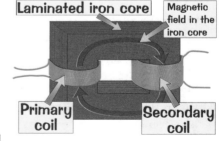

Laminated iron core / Magnetic field in the iron core / Primary coil / Secondary coil

Four Factors Affect The Size of the Induced Voltage:

This stuff <u>always</u> come up in exams. Learn them.

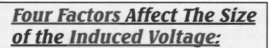

1) The <u>strength</u> of the <u>magnet</u>
2) The <u>area</u> of the <u>coil</u>
3) The <u>number of turns</u> on the <u>coil</u>
4) The <u>speed</u> of movement

'The Rate of Change of Flux' — pretty tricky isn't it...

'Electromagnetic Induction' gets my vote for 'Definitely Most Trickiest Topic in GCSE Double Science'. If it wasn't so important maybe you wouldn't have to bother learning it. The trouble is this is how all our electricity is generated. So it's pretty important. <u>Learn and scribble</u>...

The National Grid

1) The <u>National Grid</u> is the <u>network</u> of pylons and cables which <u>covers</u> the whole country.
2) It takes electricity from the <u>power stations</u>, to just where it's needed in <u>homes</u> and <u>industry</u>.
3) It enables power to be <u>generated</u> anywhere on the grid, and to then be <u>supplied</u> anywhere else on the grid.

All Power Stations are Pretty Much the Same

They all have a <u>boiler</u> of some sort, which makes <u>steam</u> which drives a <u>turbine</u> which drives a <u>generator</u>. The generator produces <u>electricity</u> (by <u>induction</u>) by <u>rotating</u> an <u>electromagnet</u> within coils of wire (see P. 103).

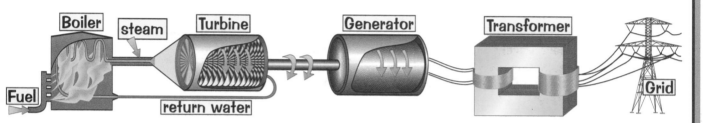

<u>Learn</u> all these features of the <u>national grid</u> — power stations, transformers, pylons, etc:

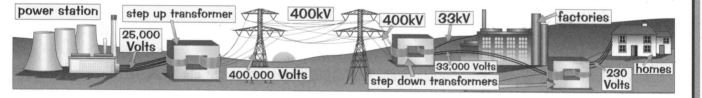

Pylon Cables are at 400,000 V to keep the Current Low

You need to understand why the <u>voltage</u> is so <u>high</u> and why it's <u>AC</u>. Learn these points.

1) The formula for <u>power supplied</u> is: <u>Power = Voltage × Current</u> or: <u>P = V×I</u>
2) So to transmit a <u>lot</u> of power, you either need high <u>voltage</u> or high <u>current</u>.
3) The problem with <u>high current</u> is the <u>loss</u> (as heat) due to the <u>resistance</u> of the cables.
4) The formula for <u>power loss</u> due to resistance in the cables is: $P = I^2R$.
5) Because of the I^2 bit, if the current is <u>10 times</u> bigger, the losses will be <u>100 times</u> bigger.
6) It's much <u>cheaper</u> to boost the voltage up to <u>400,000V</u> and keep the current <u>very low</u>.
7) This requires <u>transformers</u> as well as <u>big</u> pylons with <u>huge</u> insulators, but it's still <u>cheaper</u>.
8) The transformers have to <u>step</u> the voltage <u>up</u> at one end, for <u>efficient</u> transmission, and then bring it back down to <u>safe</u> useable levels at the other end.
9) This is why it has to be <u>AC</u> on the National Grid — so that the <u>transformers</u> will work!

400,000 Volts? — that could give you a bit of a buzz...

Quite a few tricky details on this page. The power station and National Grid are easy enough, but fully explaining why pylon cables are at 400,000 V is a bit trickier — but you need to learn it. When you boil the kettle, think of the route the electricity has to travel. <u>Scribble it down</u>.

Revision Summary For Module Ten

Electricity and magnetism. What fun. This is definitely Physics at its most grisly. The big problem with Physics in general is that usually there's nothing to 'see'. You're told that there's a current flowing or a magnetic field lurking, but there's nothing you can actually see with your eyes. That's what makes it so difficult. To get to grips with Physics you have to get used to learning about things which you can't see. Try these questions and see how well you're doing.

1) Describe what current, voltage and resistance are.
2) Sketch out the standard test circuit with all the details. Describe how it's used.
3) Describe how ammeters and voltmeters are positioned in a circuit.
4) Sketch the four standard V-I graphs and explain their shapes.
5) Scribble down 15 circuit symbols that you know, with their names of course.
6) Sketch a typical series circuit and say why it is a series circuit, not a parallel one.
7) State five rules about the current, voltage and resistance in a series circuit.
8) What is the rule for cells in series?
9) Write down the three formulae for voltage, current and resistance in a series circuit.
10) Give examples of lights wired in series and wired in parallel and explain the main differences.
11) Sketch a typical parallel circuit, showing voltmeter and ammeter positions.
12) State five rules about the current, voltage and resistance in a parallel circuit.
13) Write down the two formulas for voltage, resistance and current in a parallel circuit.
    Why is resistance so tricky?
14) Draw a circuit diagram of part of a car's electrics, and explain why they are in parallel.
15) Sketch the four important V-I graphs and explain their shapes. How do you get R from them?
16) Find the voltage when a current of 0.5 A flows through a resistance of 10 Ω.
17) What carries current in metals?
18) Draw a diagram of electrolysis in action and explain how it works.
19) What two things cause the build up of matter at the electrodes to increase?
20) What is static electricity? What is nearly always the cause of it building up?
21) Which particles move when static builds up, and which ones don't?
22) Describe how these machine use static electricity: a) inkjet printer b) photocopier.
23) Give *one* example of static being: a) a little joker b) terrorist.
24) Write down six electrical hazards in the home.
25) Sketch a properly wired plug. Explain how fuses work.
26) Explain fully how earthing works.
27) What are the four types of energy that electricity can easily be converted into?
28) Calculate the fuse rating for a toaster rated at 240 V, 0.5 kW.
29) Write down some examples of energy transfer to components in a circuit.
30) Sketch magnetic fields for: a) a bar magnet,   b) a solenoid, c) two magnets attracting,
    d) two magnets repelling, e) the Earth's magnetic field, f) a current-carrying wire.
31) What's the Right Hand Rule for?
32) What is an electromagnet made of? Explain how to decide on the polarity of the ends.
33) How do you increase the strength of an electromagnet? (Give all three answers.)
34) Sketch two demonstrations of the motor effect.
35) If the wire is placed at 45° to the magnetic field, will it experience the full force?
36) Explain two ways to reverse the direction of the force.
37) Sketch a simple motor and list the four factors which speed up the motor.
38) Describe the three details of Fleming's Left Hand Rule. What is it used for?
39) Sketch and give details of: a) Loudspeaker, b) Circuit breaker, c) Relay, d) Electric bell.
40) Give the definition of electromagnetic induction. Sketch three cases where it happens.
41) List the four factors which affect the size of the induced voltage.
42) Sketch a typical power station, and the National Grid and explain why it's at 400 kV.

Index

Index